Cooking Up Library Programs Teens and 'Tweens Will Love

Recent Titles in
Libraries Unlimited Professional Guides for Young Adult Librarians
C. Allen Nichols and Mary Anne Nichols, Series Editors

Visual Media for Teens: Creating and Using a Teen-Centered Film Collection
Jane Halsall and R. William Edminster

Teen-Centered Library Service: Putting Youth Participation into Practice
Diane P. Tuccillo

Booktalking with Teens
Kristine Mahood

Make Room for Teens!: Reflections on Developing Teen Spaces in Libraries
Michael G. Farrelly

Teens, Libraries, and Social Networking: What Librarians Need to Know
Denise E. Agosto and June Abbas, Editors

Starting from Scratch: Building a Teen Library Program
Sarah Ludwig

Serving Teen Parents: From Literacy Skills to Life Skills
Ellin Klor and Sarah Lapin

Teens Go Green!: Tips, Techniques, Tools, and Themes in YA Programming
Valerie Colston

Serving Latino Teens
Salvador Avila

Better Serving Teens through School Library–Public Library Collaborations
Cherie P. Pandora and Stacey Hayman

Teen Games Rule! A Librarian's Guide to Platforms and Programs
Julie Scordato and Ellen Forsyth, Editors

Dragons in the Stacks: A Teen Librarian's Guide to Tabletop Role-Playing
Steven A. Torres-Roman and Cason E. Snow

COOKING UP LIBRARY PROGRAMS TEENS AND 'TWEENS WILL LOVE

Recipes for Success

Megan Emery Schadlich

Foreword by Justin Hoenke

Libraries Unlimited Professional Guides for Young Adult Librarians
C. Allen Nichols and Mary Anne Nichols, Series Editors

LIBRARIES
UNLIMITED™
An Imprint of ABC-CLIO, LLC
Santa Barbara, California • Denver, Colorado

Library of Congress Cataloging-in-Publication Data

Schadlich, Megan Emery.
   Cooking up library programs teens and 'tweens will love : recipes for success / Megan Emery Schadlich ; foreword by Justin Hoenke.
      pages cm. — (Libraries unlimited professional guides for young adult librarians series)
   Includes bibliographical references and index.
   ISBN 978-1-61069-961-7 (paperback) — ISBN 978-1-61069-962-4 (ebook) 1. Young adults' libraries—Activity programs—United States. 2. Children's libraries—Activity programs—United States. 3. Libraries and teenagers—United States. I. Title.
   Z718.5.S38 2015
   027.62'60973—dc23   2015009109

ISBN: 978-1-61069-961-7
EISBN: 978-1-61069-962-4

19 18 17 16 15   1 2 3 4 5

This book is also available on the World Wide Web as an eBook.
Visit www.abc-clio.com for details.

Libraries Unlimited
An Imprint of ABC-CLIO, LLC

ABC-CLIO, LLC
130 Cremona Drive, P.O. Box 1911
Santa Barbara, California 93116-1911

This book is printed on acid-free paper ∞
Manufactured in the United States of America

CONTENTS

Series Foreword   vii

Foreword by Justin Hoenke   ix

Acknowledgments   xi

Introduction   xiii

1	Antiprogramming	1
2	Rainbow Looms for All Ages, Abilities, and Incomes	15
3	Disgusting Science	29
4	DIY Modern Crafts	47
5	The 3 Ds of 3D Printing	59
6	'Tween Lego Club	71
7	*Star Wars* Cooking Club	83
8	CSI Science	99
9	A New Take on Teen Advisory	113
10	Movie Release Events	123
11	Teen Opportunities Fair	143
12	Sewing Machine Camp	159

Index   177

SERIES FOREWORD

Programming has long been an important component of teen library services. Approaches to programming have changed over the years, and they continue to evolve. Trendy program ideas come and go while tried and true programming stays the same—or is revived with a twist. But one thing remains the same: teens and teen librarians love it! Megan Emery Schadlich has provided a recipe for program success that will give new teen librarians a place to start and experienced librarians renewed energy and ideas. Megan's enthusiasm for working with teens shines through in her ideas and delivery of programs. She has provided easy-to-follow step-by-step instructions so that anyone can replicate these programs in his or her own library. Ideas can also be personalized to fit your own communities. As a bonus, she has provided tie-ins to STEM (science, technology, engineering, and math) and STEAM (science, technology, engineering, art, and math) initiatives and addresses how you can attract both 'tweens and teens.

We are proud of our association with Libraries Unlimited/ABC-CLIO, which continues to prove itself the premier publisher of books to help library staff serve teens. This series has succeeded because our authors know the needs of those library employees who work with teens. Without exception, they have written useful and practical handbooks for library staff.

We hope that you find this book, as well as our entire series, to be informative, that it provides you with valuable ideas as you serve teens, and that it will further inspire you to do great things to make teens welcome in your library. If you have an idea for a title that could be added to our series or would like to submit a book proposal, please e-mail us at bittner@abc -clio.com. We'd love to hear from you.

Mary Anne Nichols
C. Allen Nichols
Series Editors

FOREWORD

Once upon a time Benjamin Franklin got together with a bunch of his friends and created the Junto, a group of like-minded community members. In what was most likely a really fancy and elegant British accent, he suggested to his friends that they should all pool their resources (which back in that day were pretty much just books) and share ideas. From the Junto began the Library Company of Philadelphia, an organization that still exists to this day to help the community learn, grow, and share ideas.

How does this have anything to do with the book you're about to read? Well, for all of this to make sense, we have to ask ourselves a question. What's at the core of the Junto? The easy answer would be books. But books are just a small part of the answer. The core of the Junto was people—people coming together to share ideas and resources and to better serve the community.

Much like the Junto, the second floor of the downtown Chattanooga Public Library was created to share ideas and resources and to better serve the youth and family community of Chattanooga, Tennessee. This is the place where Megan Emery Schadlich, your author and new best friend over the next 140 or so pages, spends her days. During her time on the second floor, Megan has developed and implemented many programs for kids, 'tweens, teens, and families. These programs, focused on providing the community with an experience that smooshes together both learning and fun, have given the Chattanooga community a library that allows them to explore the world around them. But once again I ask you to think about what's at the core of the second floor. Is it technology, like Arduinos and littleBits? Is it crafting supplies, like wool, felt, and yarn? No. All of those things help make the second floor an awesome place for kids, 'tweens, teens, and families, but at the core of the second floor is the same thing that was at the core of the Junto: people.

In this book, Megan gives public libraries the Batman-esque utility belt full of ideas, tools, and inspiration that they need to go out and connect with their 'tween and teen communities. When you, oh awesome reader of this book, strap on this utility belt and head out into your library with a head full of ideas and a heart full of inspiration, you will connect with your community. You will bring the people in your community together inside the most wonderful and amazing institution that human beings have ever created: the public library.

On a personal note: Megan, I'm so happy that you went to the same school as my wife and that your brother was in her class and then randomly about five years later you met me and my wife when we lived in Maine. We connected and then somehow we all ended up working in the same library in Chattanooga, Tennessee. I am very proud of you.

Justin Hoenke
Chattanooga, Tennessee

ACKNOWLEDGMENTS

This book was a labor of love only made possible because of the support of my husband, Karl, who put up with my sleepless nights, took over the housework, and ordered me pizza so I wouldn't have to cook. I promise to keep my light shining brightest for you.

My high standards and inspiration come from the honesty and friendship of all the kids I've been so lucky to work with.

My father taught me to be strong in my convictions and my mother taught me to truly be myself no matter how weird I seemed in comparison to others. You were right, Mom. Those really are the best parts.

My competitive nature was turned into a force for good by my best friends Christine Balch, Jessica Goodman, and Gretchen Tucker. No longer must I win all the board games; I can simply change the world for good.

All of this manifested in libraries because my coworkers took a risk on a passionate kid advocate who didn't have the right degree but never stops thinking about libraries. Again and again you have trusted my crazy ideas and given me the support to try something new. Also, you all said no to fire in the library. Now I see that that was the right choice. Jill Tofferi, Ginger Palmer, David Moorhead, Rick Spears, Marcela Peres, Grace Green, Amy Howlett, Mara Siegel, Justin Hoenke, Meg Backus, Mary Barnett, Corinne Hill, Nate Hill, Jessica Cooley Meyer, and Sarah Anne Brewer, you are the tip of the iceberg of brilliant, talented people I've been lucky enough to work with.

My editors, Barbara Ittner and MaryAnne Nichols, helped keep the book sounding like me while somehow getting it organized at the same time. We'll look at my closets next, ladies . . .

There are so many other people who have impacted me, too many to name. I love you all and can't wait to see what adventures we create next!

INTRODUCTION

The landscape of our profession is one of constant change. We juggle collection development that reflects our audiences while learning and teaching how to download music, books, and movies to the latest devices. We craft community partnerships with one hand and tackle policy development with the other. When the stars align perfectly we do all this *and* offer high-quality programming reflective of national trends that relate to each of our neighborhoods, cities, small towns, schools, and more.

This book is a collection of tried-and-true successful programs I've run in libraries across the United States, from a small ski town in Vermont to a small city in Maine and finally to my current mid-sized city of Chattanooga, Tennessee. I know you can find success with them because I already have—over and over again.

The book's format is that of a cookbook, something we're all pretty familiar with. The amount of money and work that goes into each program varies so that there's something for the librarian with no time and no budget and something for the librarian who's ready to carve out a chunk of time to create a larger-than-life event. You can read through the book from cover to cover or randomly skip about and find something that works for you.

I hope the book gives you some new programs your 'tweens and teens will love as much as mine do; but, more importantly, I hope it inspires you to get creative, talk with your audience, and create your own wacky and wild programs. Each of us is in a one-of-a-kind environment that deserves to be reflected in our programming, and I know you'll find a way to honor and inspire what is uniquely you!

1

◇ ◇ ◇

ANTIPROGRAMMING

When scheduling events, conflicts invariably arise. Teens, 'tweens, and their families have busier schedules than ever, and making it to your event simply may not be feasible. However, if you can leave an event up all week and on display for people to access at their leisure, not only will they get a taste of all the cool things you're doing but it will also be at a time that is convenient for them. They'll get used to the idea of the library being a place they can come for great experiences as well as materials, no matter what time of day works for them. That's the beauty of antiprogramming.

It's simple to start antiprogramming (sometimes referred to as "unprogramming" or "passive programming"), and while the ideas laid out in this chapter are successfully engaging our patrons in Chattanooga, you can start in a much simpler way by using up those random materials you inherited with your job or that someone helpfully donated and that you can't figure out how to get rid of!

Think of antiprogramming areas as fun, messy zones that act as informal makerspaces. They will draw people into your library and can have a big impact on your program attendance statistics. Keep track of those numbers, because libraries are turning into places where our equipment is less for us to become masters of (and slaves to!) and more for our patrons to utilize. Your statistics will show a need for continued growth in your equipment and programming budgets that will support the work you're doing.

STOCKING THE PANTRY

- Instagram Photo Booth
  - iPad

- o Box to secure
  - Build or buy your booth! A Google or Pinterest search will return a ton of results, but keep in mind you want a vertical angle of 90 degrees for customer convenience. If you have a volunteer or employee who is handy at woodworking you are ready to go.
  - o Apps to take pictures (e.g., Photobooth or Pocketbooth)
  - o Fun paper backdrops you make yourself (think seasonal or themed around a hot new book release)
  - o Table and a chair or two
- Button Maker
  - o Button maker (see the Recipes section for examples)
  - o Discarded periodicals—especially those with lots of color pictures
  - o Circle cutter
  - o Table and chairs
- Buddha Board
  - o Buddha Board
  - o Water
  - o Table and chair
- Yarn Bombing
  - o Table and chairs
  - o Yarn
  - o Knitting needles
  - o Crochet hooks
- Art Station
  - o Table and chairs
  - o Paper
  - o Scrap paper
  - o Colored pencils, markers, and/or crayons
  - o Scissors
  - o Glue sticks
  - o Tracer table or light box
  - o Spiral graph
- The Random Table of Who Knows What—or, you've already got what you need!
  - o Paper (even your ugly paper and the bigger the better!)
  - o Crayons, markers, or colored pencils
  - o Stickers
  - o Random craft supplies you don't know what to do with
  - o The weird stuff people donate that you think you'll never use (old plastic toys, random craft supplies, puzzles, board games, etc.)
  - o Discarded books and periodicals
  - o Discarded furniture or office materials
  - o Boxes

Feel free to reach out to your patrons or local organizations for materials. Writing grants for these antiprogramming makerspaces is also a good idea. The materials for these areas are inexpensive to purchase but will have a BIG impact on your attendance statistics. That's a recipe for success that granting committees love!

PROMOTING YOUR PROGRAM

Word-of-mouth promotion does wonders for these programs. Once people get used to the idea of the library as a center for activities, they'll swing by regularly to see what's new.

In the beginning, promote with your regular posters. In addition to hanging posters, focus on promoting the fact that people can drop in whenever they want to participate. Also, when you're talking to patrons about donating materials, let your excitement over this new program show! Your enthusiasm is contagious and will draw a better crowd than any poster ever could!

RECIPES

Instagram Photo Booth

While photo booths aren't a new idea, the way they're executed creates an opportunity for digital creation rather than just digital consumption. The many filters available in apps make the photos look different in dozens of ways and provide a fascinating window into the individuality and self-expression of 'tweens and teens. To top it all off, using tech equipment like an iPad supports our goal of bridging the digital divide in a new, fun way, as opposed to one with an educational undertone that many kids turn their noses up at (or try to change). Enjoy the silliness of this program and incorporate it into other things you do, like having participants take a photo of their finished products after a craft class or stop-animating a short video!

Here's a link to the Pinterest board where I keep track of all my ideas for my own Instagram photo booth: http://www.pinterest.com/bibliochica /create-a-photobooth/. And here's a link to our second-floor photo booth at the Chattanooga Public Library: http://instagram.com/2ndFloorPhoto Booth.

Tab Indicators

STEAM
- S: Experimenting with cameras and filters, testing different apps
- T: Using equipment: iPad and apps

E: Posing and adjusting photos to fit in a frame

A: Making faces, posing for photos, choosing filters to complete photo composition

M: Gauging the distance from the lens and positioning for photo composition

Time

5 to 10 minutes (just setup, posting photos, and the occasional instruction)

Age level

All ages

Ingredients

- iPad
- Box to secure
  - Build a booth
    - http://www.instructables.com/id/Make-Your-Own-Table top-Photobooth/
  - Buy a booth
    - A Google search will provide a ton of results. Take the time and discuss with your staff what your best choice is.
    - Here's one example: http://www.apgexhibits.com/Counter top-and-Wall-Mount-iPad-Display-Stand-p/ipad-ctr-wal.htm
- Apps to take pictures
  - Some will be preloaded
  - Others can be purchased or are free:
    - Instabooth (free)
    - Pocketbooth
- Fun paper backdrops
  - Creating backdrops is a great volunteer task for your artistically-minded teens
- A table to put the iPad box on
- Silly paper props like mustaches, signs, glasses, masks, hats, etc.
- A chair or two

Setup

1. Get an iPad (you may want your tech team to lock down the iPad so all it's capable of doing is taking the photos and posting them to Instagram, but that's up to you and your policies).
2. Mount new case to table and insert iPad.
3. Download a few fun photo apps to the iPad.
4. Set up an Instagram account for the iPad or your department/library.
5. Set out your photo props.

6. Create your first fun backdrop.
7. Have a seat, play with the apps, take some photos, and post them to Instagram!

Instructions

1. Leave instructions on how to use the Photobooth.
2. Let it do its magic!
3. Every now and then, you'll need to review and post a couple of new photos to Instagram and erase all the extras that were taken and aren't the best. Keep in mind you don't want your photos to become spam; posting two every hour or so is plenty.
4. In a month or two you'll want to change your backdrop to reflect a new program or season, or get creative and give your teens some artistic freedom. You'll love what they come up with!

Button Maker

The button-making station is one of the busiest areas in the Chattanooga Public Library at any given time. Teens huddle and produce dozens at a time, families come in and create buttons together, presents are made to ship to faraway friends and family members. For the amount it costs, a lot less than the cost of a performer, you can have a yearlong program that draws in tons of teens, 'tweens, and their families. It's a no-brainer!

Our favorite is the 1" button maker that makes those great punk rock–sized pins, so that's what I'll be referencing here.

Tab Indicators

STEAM

S: Experimenting with images to create buttons
T: Using equipment: button maker, circle cutter
E: Constructing buttons, learning workings of machinery
A: Creating artwork to turn into buttons, repurposing art from periodicals into buttons
M: Gauging appropriately sized artwork for buttons, creating appropriately sized artwork for buttons

Time

No time (only setup and occasional instruction)

Age level

All ages (though children under 8 will need adult supervision)

Ingredients

- Button maker
  - The sturdiest button maker around comes from American Button Machine, plus they have a support line you can call for help if it gets jammed. A starter kit will have everything you need: http://www.americanbuttonmachines.com/product/1-beginner-button-making-kit/
  - Or you can buy the button maker only: http://www.americanbuttonmachines.com/product/1-button-machine/
- Circle cutter
  - Again, American Button Machine has a great circle cutter that's sturdy. It comes in the starter kit, or you can purchase a replacement on its own: http://www.americanbuttonmachines.com/product/circle-cutter/
- Steel plate
  - This also comes in the starter kit, or you can purchase a replacement plate on its own: http://www.americanbuttonmachines.com/product/replacement-cutting-plate/
- Button-making supplies
  - Enough supplies for 250 buttons will come in your starter kit from American Button Machine, but replacement materials are available.
    - Complete button-making sets (for 500 buttons) are also available: http://www.americanbuttonmachines.com/product/1-pinback-button-set/
    - Additional Mylar covers may be purchased in sets of 1,000: http://www.americanbuttonmachines.com/product/1-round-mylar/
    - Scrap paper
    - Colored pencils, markers, and/or crayons
    - Discarded periodicals
- Containers for button-making supplies
  - Simple plastic bowls or jars will work to hold your
    - Metal rings
    - Metal coin pieces
    - Pinbacks
    - Mylar covers
    - Free buttons

Setup

1. Grab a table, and place it where you want your button-making station.
2. Arrange your button maker and button-making supplies in their containers on top of the table.

3. Make a few buttons to kick off your new station and place them in a "free button bin."

Instructions

1. When you look at the button machine, notice that there is a shallow end on the left-hand side and a deep end on the right-hand side. Insert your coin piece flat side up in the shallow end on the left, like an upside down cup.
2. Place your artwork on top of the coin piece so that you can see the picture you want.
3. Place a Mylar sheet on top of your artwork.
4. In the deep end place one of the metal rings, flat side down this time.
5. Pivot your artwork underneath the large metal circle until it won't spin any more.
6. Pull the handle of the button maker down and toward you. Use your muscles!
7. Pull the handle of the button maker back up into its starting position.
8. Make sure your metal ring is lying flat in the deep end and then pivot it under the large metal circle until it won't spin any more. You won't see your artwork any more, but don't worry, this is simply the magic of the button maker!
9. Pull the handle of the button maker down and toward you again—remember, muscles!
10. Pull the handle of the button maker back up into its starting position.
11. Pivot the shallow end back underneath the large metal circle to reveal your button!
12. To insert your pinback, hold it like a rainbow, arched, and with the squiggle on the left-hand side.
13. Feed the squiggle into the back of your button under the metal lip.
14. Push in and down until the pinback snaps into place.
15. Voila! Button!
16. If you like your button, keep it or give it to a friend. If you decide you don't like how it turned out, leave it in the free button bin for someone else to enjoy!

Buddha Board

Another inexpensive way to start antiprogramming is by using a Buddha Board, which is a simple piece of "Magic Paper" mounted to a black background. The mounted paper sits atop a simple black tray that holds water and a Japanese calligraphy brush. You paint the water onto the paper, creating a dramatic calligraphy-style stroke mark that appears as though you dipped your brush in black ink. After a few minutes the image evaporates and disappears from the paper. A Buddha Board is powerful in two ways. First, it holds a lot of that wow-factor magic in that the paintings you create on it disappear before your eyes, making it almost impossible not to play with. Second, it holds therapeutic benefits when you pair its wow factor with the Zen idea of living in the moment. It's important to let kids know that it's all right to feel sad or angry, as long as they can release it in a healthy way. The Buddha Board is one fabulous release for these emotions. Kids can literally paint away their troubles by creating an artistic image of whatever is bugging them and watching it fade away. Let them know that once it's gone from the board they should let it slide away from their minds as well.

Tab Indicators

STEAM

S: Experimenting with brush strokes and brushes
T: Using equipment
E: Creating paintings
A: Painting
M:

Time

5 to 10 minutes (Only setup plus occasional instruction)

Age level

All ages

Ingredients

- Buddha Board
  - Buy it at http://buddhaboard.com/
  - Make your own: http://www.ehow.com/how_7770787_make-buddha-board.html
  - Experiment with Magic Water Painting Paper or Magic Water Painting Cloth. A Google search reveals many purchasing options.
- Extra paintbrushes
- Water
- Table and chair

Setup

1. Place table and chair(s) in an area where it's safe to play with a little water (1 cup or less).

2. Arrange the Buddha Board on the table.
3. Fill the Buddha Board base with water.
4. Leave out extra paintbrushes for experimentation with brush strokes, if desired.
5. Put up a sign with the instructions listed below.
6. Make a painting of your own!

Instructions

1. Choose your brush.
2. Dip it in water.
3. Express yourself!
4. Let your troubles melt away.

Yarn Bombing

Yarn bombing is when you take an object that is not a piece of art (a tree, chalkboard, parking meter, etc.) and wrap it in knitted or crocheted pieces you made, turning it into an art installation piece. Yarn seems to be one of those craft items people are always so thrilled to give away to someone who will appreciate or use it. If you're like most folks, you've got dozens of skeins squirreled away for whatever craft might arise. If not, lucky for you because it's inexpensive and you probably have patrons who would be happy to donate to your new program!

Yarn bombing is such a hot form of public art these days that it's almost a no-brainer. It's a great way to appeal to teens and 'tweens while spreading the yarn-bombing idea that anything can become art. In addition, it's easy to teach a few basic crochet tricks that will get kids started; and leaving out tools for them to experiment with will grab their attention once their curiosity is piqued!

Tab Indicators

STEAM

S: Experimenting with crochet and knitting techniques, crochet hooks, knitting needles, and alternative crochet hooks or knitting needles

T: Using knitting and crochet equipment and 3D printed knitting needles or crochet hooks

E: Creating fabric arts materials, engineering yarn pieces, constructing yarn bomb finished products

A: Designing overall yarn-bombing project, making creative yarn-bomb pieces

M: Following patterns, counting stitches/rows, measuring the object to be bombed, calculating how much yarn will be needed to complete a bomb

Time

5 to 10 minutes (only setup and occasional instruction)

Age level

8 to 18 years

Ingredients

- Table and chairs
- Jars/cans
- Yarn
- Knitting needles
- Crochet hooks
- Chopsticks
- Pencils

Setup

1. Arrange the table in a place where kids can hang out, laugh, and have fun without being in the way or disturbing others.
2. Pile yarn in a variety of colors on top of the table.
3. Arrange jars or cans filled with knitting needles, crochet hooks, pencils, or chopsticks in whatever combination pleases you.
4. Place a sign on the table with instructions on how to crochet using just your fingers but expect to get asked for hands-on instruction! (Here are some well-written instructions: http://www.ehow.com/how_6132720_finger-crochet-instructions.html; and here's a helpful video: https://www.youtube.com/watch?v=AEo2xG25Uro.)
5. Make a few starter crocheted chains for examples or for kids to practice on until they have the hang of it.
6. If you have the time, finish off a few chains and start yarn bombing something in your area (a book cart, signpost, door handle, etc.) as an example of what a finished product can look like!

Instructions

1. Show off the table to kids coming into the library and get them engaged!
2. Pick up your started crochet chain and demonstrate how easy it is, then ask if the kids want to try it on your chain.
3. Once they're hooked, encourage them to start their own chain.
4. Once they get a nice long chain they may want to bring it home instead of donating it to your yarn-bomb project. Let them. Yarn is

cheap, and it'll build good will. Next time they come in ask if they'll be contributing to the yarn bomb that day, or if they've yarn bombed anything at home with what they created last time!

To crochet chains:

When starting out, a thicker, chunkier yarn is easier to learn with and will create a chain faster, allowing kids to make progress more quickly, achieve gratification faster, and hook them on this craft. (Pun totally intended.)

1. Tie a knot with a loop onto the end of your yarn.
2. Place two fingers through the loop.
3. Pull your yarn through the loop.
4. Make the loop snug.
5. Place two fingers through your new loop. Repeat!

To bomb an object:

Start simple and choose an object that is more square in shape and less wavy. Things like table legs, lamps, or chair backs all work well.

1. Start at the base of the object.
2. Wrap your chain around the object once.
3. Tie a tight knot around the object.
4. Start wrapping your chain around the object in an upward spiral.
5. Wrapping loosely or tightly will create different looks, so experiment.
6. When you reach the end of your chain, have a friend tie his or her chain onto yours or start at different points and see what happens when it meets up in the middle!

Going further:

1. Make some pompoms to tie onto your chains and see how the look changes.
2. Try sewing your chains together into large pieces to wrap around and sew onto objects.
3. Get technical and measure an object to create a custom-fit yarn bomb.
4. Learn advanced designs, like daisy chains, and create some vines to yarn bomb with.
5. Create your own patterns and designs. One local teen came up with the idea of yarn-bombing rocks to distribute all over the city.

Art Station

An art station is probably the simplest station to put together and the most tried and true, an art station can truly be anything. Throw down a huge piece of paper with the words "Doodle on me!" in a fun lettering.

Start some doodles, then watch kids add to it and go bananas. Throw out some random art supplies with a sign that challenges kids to "Make something!" and see what clever creations they come up with! Or get more advanced and add some equipment like a light box or a spiral graph and take it to a new level involving equipment and an engineering focus.

Tab Indicators

STEAM

    S: Experimenting with tracing techniques, experimenting with patterns

    T: Using equipment: tracing tables, spiral graphs, multiple art mediums

    E: Replicating drawings or photos with hand drawings

    A: Practicing drawing styles of other artists, creating new pieces of art, combining multiple mediums into one piece of art

    M: Following patterns, creating patterns

Time

5 to 10 minutes (only setup and occasional instruction)

Age level

2 to 18 years

Ingredients

- Table and chairs
- Paper
- Scrap paper
- Colored pencils, markers, and/or crayons
- Scissors
- Glue sticks
- Pencil sharpener(s)
- Trash and/or recycling bin
- Tracer Table or Light Box
  - Buy one: They are available online at http://www.artsupply.com/Artograph-Light-Tracer-10X12_p_45979.html
  - Or make your own! See http://www.teachpreschool.org/2012/01/guest-post-a-homemade-light-table-for-preschool/
- Spiral graph
  - Check out this cool 3D version available online: http://www.onlinesciencemall.com/3d-art-creative-spiral-fun-graphing.html?utm_source=gpla&utm_campaign=ProductListingAds&

gclid=CjwKEAjw0a2eBRDVrabv9vWJ90USJACsKRDHPrHSjx
Mpsf6gsf-QmhDoYGgPyB6Rcd72Ruzy01Z33hoCxa7w_wcB

Setup

1. Set up your table and chairs in a place where kids can get creative (and a little bit messy). If you plan on using the Light Box or the kind of pencil sharpener you have to plug in, be sure you're near an outlet.
2. Arrange your fun new station however you like! This zone will get messy with art supplies scattered around, but that's part of what makes it so inviting for kids! Seeing a spot where they can engage in some messy, creative play is appealing and will help promote this area.
3. If you are using the Light Box you may want to print out some images for the kids to trace. Just think about what they're into, whether it's cartoons, comic books, or games, and use those. Or even better, ask them what they want!

Instructions

1. Let kids play!
2. Be prepared to show them how to use the spiral graph and light table and how to print some more images.

The Random Table of Who Knows What!

We've all received those donations that instantly made us think "What on earth am I going to do with this???" This table is your answer. This is where you'll put out your random toys to be played with until they die (even if that's just a few days), the ugly thread no one will ever choose for their sewing projects (let's make worry dolls!), the donation of 10,000 foam stars (learn to make constellation mobiles!), *Reader's Digest* magazines from the mid-1970s (create a collage!), and so on . . .

Librarians are notorious hoarders. Do yourself a favor and clear out that back closet so you can use the place for more important things. After all, aren't we saving them for the perfect opportunity to let the kids play with them? Do it this way and get some amazing statistics out of them!

RESOURCES

Here's a fabulous rundown of resources from the great Amy Koester and Marge Loch-Wouters on unprogramming: http://showmelibrarian.blogspot.com/2013/07/unprogramming-part-i-programming.html.

Tips and Tricks

The ideas listed here work well in my current library, but that doesn't mean they'll be a perfect fit for you. If your antiprograms aren't taking off the way you hope, consider getting your community's input during a focus group as described in the chapter "A New Take on the Teen Advisory."

These small stations are a great way to try new fads and get the most bang for your buck. Frequently we purchase the hot new toy only to have it sit on a shelf and be pulled out only when we can control all aspects of its use. Rainbow Looms are a perfect example. The library world was all atwitter when these toys came out: "How can we use these?" "What can we make with them?" "What's the potential of this?" "Is it a toy or a tool?" By simply putting it out for your kids to experiment with you can learn the answers to all these questions and many more you didn't even think of!

In the next chapter we'll take a look at how to run a Rainbow Loom antiprogram and other programs that grew out of simply letting kids play with these awesome toys. (Or are they tools???)

2

◇ ◇ ◇

RAINBOW LOOMS FOR ALL AGES, ABILITIES, AND INCOMES

Rainbow Looms—designed by a crash safety engineer at Nissan, initially recognized as "brilliant" by Learning Express Toys, then launched into toy superstardom by Michaels craft stores—are definitely one of the hottest items in library land right now. They're priced inexpensively, fit well with the maker movement, don't take up much space, and are an easy fit for STEAM programming!

The idea is simple: you stretch small colorful rubber bands across pegs in different patterns and then use a hook to pull the rubber bands over one another, linking them together and completing the design. When you pull the rubber bands off the pegs you've got a colorful piece of artwork to wear or give to a friend. You can use Rainbow Looms to make bracelets, necklaces, charms, zipper pulls, rings, toys, bags, and more!

The Internet is littered with tutorials of industrious 'tweens and teens who have taken the basic equipment and reinvented how to use it and what they can create. Some have even abandoned the loom and found new ways to get creative! The projects are also easy to learn and 'tweens and teens are quick to grab a laptop, learn something new, and show it off to friends or offer to teach a newbie the ropes. One of the best things about Rainbow Looms is their diversity. They're great for making so much more than bracelets, and both boys and girls love to create using them!

In addition to providing almost effortless programming, Rainbow Looms are ideal for a fun introductory volunteer experience that can lead to a more invested volunteer down the line. My teens can't believe it when I tell them they can earn community service hours by hanging out with other kids and playing on the looms. Teens and 'tweens already possess this skill, so that means you don't have to learn all those tricky designs yourself, and giving them the responsibility for teaching others shows that you value their knowledge and talents.

To get started you can simply go the antiprogramming route and leave the looms out on a table. Newbies and younger kids may ask you how to make simple bracelets, and the older or more experienced kids will probably just sit down and go to town. It doesn't have to stop there though. You can step up your game by offering specialty classes and bands specifically purchased for cool designs. Host contests and encourage kids to post their own tutorials and instructional videos. These little wonders can help you incorporate even more tech and expand the range of STEAM connections.

Whichever route you choose, take the time to learn a few cool, trick designs and your 'tweens and teens will appreciate your shared interest. Then build programs around your new abilities!

STOCKING THE PANTRY

- A Rainbow Loom Starter Kit (at Rainbowloom.com) includes
  - One Rainbow Loom (you'll want one per person)
  - One Mini Rainbow Loom
  - One metal hook
  - 600 latex-free rubber bands
  - 1 bag of C-clips
  - Instructional manual to learn simple bracelets
- Replacement bands are available in bags of 600 on Rainbowloom .com, or you can buy knockoff brands on Amazon.com or other sites.
- C-clips can be printed using a 3D printer if you have one. If you have a MakerBot just do a search for them on Thingiverse.com to see your options! If you don't have a 3D printer, you can purchase bags of 96 refill C-clips on Rainbowloom.com, or inexpensive knockoffs can be found on Amazon.com and similar sites. These are sometimes called C-clips but can also be called S-clips and will be (you guessed it!) S-shaped instead of C-shaped.
- Aluminum jump rings are used in some tutorials, and a few hundred can be purchased on Amazon.com or through other sources you can find through a basic Web search. You'll want to use a size between 15 and 18 gauge.

- For alternative Rainbow Looms, you can use push pins in wood or wine corks, plastic forks with the center tines broken out, or your fingers!

PROMOTING YOUR PROGRAM

To be honest, the looms themselves will do a lot of the work. Once kids know they're available they'll gain their own little following! However, here are some ideas to get you off the ground.

- Print out some cardstock cards with info about your new Rainbow Loom club, Rainbow Loom classes, or their general availability, and attach some bracelets to the cards. Give them away at your special events to promote any aspect of new Rainbow Loom activities you'd like to highlight!
- Display the cards (or the looms) front and center, where people can see them as they come into the library or your department or area. You want people to ask what they are and then spread the word that your library is now among the ranks of the hip, cool places in town that support all things Rainbow Loom! Don't forget, word of mouth is still the best form of publicity, so let your patrons know how excited you are about the looms, whether that's parents, grand-parents, or the 'tweens and teens themselves!
- Host a kickoff contest with a prize of rubber bands, library fine for-giveness, a Rainbow Loom book, or something else unique to your location. (This can be a great way to locate your Rainbow Loom volunteers also!) Your contest could be for the coolest design, the longest chain made in a set amount of time, or something more com-plicated—like seeing who can re-create the library logo.
- Promote your looms at other events you host, and build off their success.
  - Do you have a Minecraft group? Make some Creepers to give away, and then teach a tutorial class down the line!
  - Do you know some American Girl doll enthusiasts? Host a class to make items like shoes, jewelry, or pets for the dolls!
  - Give away some cool stuff made on your Rainbow Loom during school visits as a way to talk up the program and pique the kids' interest.
  - Celebrate holidays by releasing rubber bands in cool new colors. Think Halloween, Mardi Gras, 4th of July, Valentine's Day, and other non–gender-based or non–religious-based holidays—and run with it!

○ What local events are special to your geographic area? Give away items specific to those happenings!

RECIPES

Rainbow Loom Antiprogram

As stated in chapter 1, I'm a huge fan of antiprogramming. The Rainbow Loom is a natural antiprogram because it's small, it's portable, and it makes no noise—but it has big results that kids can't wait to show off. Leaving a Rainbow Loom out on a table with a few instructions or a laptop for kids to use to explore is a makerspace in itself.

Tab Indicators

STEAM

S: Experimenting with alternative materials to create new looms, experimenting with design components to create new designs
T: Using equipment, doing online research for designs and patterns
E: Creating new looms out of alternative materials, making items by hand
A: Making your own design, applying general creativity
M: Following patterns, counting rubber bands, creating patterns

Time

5 to 10 minutes (setup time only)

Age level

8 to 18 years

Ingredients

- Rainbow Loom(s) (one per person)
- Rubber bands
- C-clips
- Hooks
- Any combination of alternative Rainbow Loom materials to encourage kids to engineer their own

Setup

1. Designate a table and chairs just for the Rainbow Looms. Kids love to huddle together and work on designs, so be ready for clusters of kids.

2. Set looms, bands, C-clips, and instructions on the table.
3. If desired, set up a computer that can access YouTube so the kids can browse for designs.
4. Make a sign that lets parents know the STEAM benefits of playing with Rainbow Looms and display it proudly in your new antiprogram area!

Instructions

1. Walk away, but keep track of the people who use your new Anti-programming Station as these are powerful statistics you can use to fund more maker programs in the future!
2. Offer to help, if needed. Suggesting new YouTube tutorials and instructions will let the 'tweens and teens know you're as into the craft as they are.
3. Set out some alternative looms (see the next program recipe for ideas!).

Resources

Rainbow Loom's website (for supplies and tutorials):
http://www.rainbowloom.com/

Alternative Looms

Socioeconomic barriers create cultural rifts, and while the library can amend some of that by offering play experiences like Rainbow Looms for everyone, you can also teach your kids how to keep creating from home even if they can't afford a Rainbow Loom of their own. Alternative looms get kids thinking outside the box and looking at the world around them to see how they can turn a little bit of nothing into something. It's a great maker extension for a program that's already a maker experience, and kids can take home an alternate loom, which will let them create the same great items as the regular looms!

Tab Indicators

STEAM

S: Experimenting with alternative materials to create new looms, experimenting with design components to create new designs
T: Using equipment, doing online research for designs and patterns
E: Creating new looms out of alternative materials, making items by hand
A: Making with you own design, applying general creativity

M: Following patterns, counting rubber bands, creating patterns

Time

1 hour

Age level

8 to 18 years

Ingredients

- Pushpins that have those nice colorful plastic pushing parts (as opposed to the metal ones that lie flat when pushed in)
- Wood
- Nails
- Hammer
- Pliers
- Wine corks
- Your own hands
- Bands
- C-clips
- Hooks
- Any random extra pieces you have lying around that you think might be reimagined into a loom (think popsicle sticks, nails, chopsticks, etc.). You never know what kids might come up with!

Setup

1. Set up a table with plenty of chairs for your 'tweens and teens to gather around. Be ready for them to huddle together and abandon those chairs or to move them all over the place.
2. Before teaching any type of alternative loom, test it out to see if you can get it to work so you can offer tips to your kids.
3. Put out a couple examples of looms you made ahead of time along with all the great random supplies you've gathered.

Instructions

1. To make a wine cork loom, insert two pushpins into the side of your wine cork so they follow the grain. They should be about a half inch apart. This simple loom will create fishtail and inverted fishtail patterns.
2. To make a wooden loom, insert pushpins or, preferably, nails into your piece of wood leaving a distance of a half inch between each. Then start using your new loom just like a regular Rainbow Loom!

3. To make a hand loom, you only need your two fingers. Treat your two fingers like the two pegs of a loom and start a fishtail pattern or a beginner bracelet pattern on them!

4. Get creative! Let the kids mix and match designs, play with the random materials you gathered, and come up with something new. If you have a 3D printer you can encourage them to create a new design and then print it out.

Resources

The following YouTube tutorials give instructions on different kinds of looming:

Finger looming: https://www.youtube.com/watch?v=6NLf18NLWNw
Fork looming: https://www.youtube.com/watch?v=KLzqoNDhOL8
Wine cork looming: https://www.youtube.com/watch?v=wiBgAvtb KxU
Foot Looming: https://www.youtube.com/watch?v=8gL5K4mjG5o

Volunteer-Led Rainbow Loom Class

Teens and 'tweens usually know more about these looms than you or I will ever have time to learn. They are natural experts and as such are the perfect teachers! Teens and 'tweens *love* learning from and teaching their peers, so giving them a well-crafted volunteer opportunity to do so will up your cool points while giving them a sense of ownership of your library.

Tab Indicators

STEAM

S: Experimenting with lesson plan
T: Doing online research for designs and patterns
E: Making items by hand, crafting a lesson plan
A: Coming up with a design, applying general creativity, teaching designs to peers
M: Following patterns, counting rubber bands, creating patterns, timing a lesson plan

Time

1.5 hours

Age level

10 to 18 years

Ingredients

- Rainbow Loom(s) (one per person)
- Rubber bands
- C-clips
- Hooks
- Any combination of the alternative Rainbow Loom materials to encourage kids to engineer their own

Setup

1. Give yourself a half hour for discussion with your volunteer two weeks before the program (or whatever works for your organization in terms of sending out marketing materials) to do the following:
   - Explain how a program works at your library:
     - How long it takes to set up
     - What age range works well when it comes to Rainbow Looms
     - How much time your 'tweens and teens will sit and learn before getting distracted or bored
     - How much noise is permissible
     - Any other specifics or quirks they should keep in mind (e.g., library policies or challenges that may arise)
   - Get the volunteer to choose one or two designs and then teach you how to create them. This shows the volunteer just how long explaining actually takes, as opposed to watching and re-creating the steps they've learned on their own. It's also good practice for them to decide how they'll hold their own loom when teaching and for the two of you to determine any steps that may require extra hand-holding by class participants.
   - Once you both know the design the volunteer will be teaching and you've started your test run, break down the hour-long class time-wise into something like this:
     - 3:00–3:05: Participants arrive; make introductions.
     - 3:05–3:10: Show an example of the design they'll be learning today. Point out any areas that may cause trouble, but reassure everyone that they will leave with a completed design, or if they don't finish they can stay and keep crafting or return later if they would prefer. (This all depends on how intricate a design the volunteer will be teaching. Keep the difficulty level in mind when creating your promotional materials about the class. If it is a difficult design, you may want to state on your posters "This is an advanced-level class.")
     - 3:10–3:25: Teach steps 1 through 4 of the design, and give individual help as needed.
     - 3:25–3:50: Teach steps 5 through 10 of the design, and give individual help as needed.

- ○ 3:50–4:00: Put finishing touches on designs. The librarian invites participants who want to teach in the future to fill out and leave a volunteer application.
- ○ 4:00–4:15: Librarian and volunteer discuss what went well, what they would change, and when to do the program again!
- • Agree to a time when the volunteer will return and add that to the schedule.
2. A week before the volunteer's class, touch base with an e-mail or a phone call to make sure it's still a go and there's no need to reschedule.
3. A day before the volunteer's class, touch base once more to be sure the class will still happen.
4. Get ready to watch the magic and enjoy taking the backseat!

Instructions

1. Greet your volunteer when he or she arrives, lead the volunteer to where the class will be taught, and offer to help set up.
2. Once everything is set up for the class, give the volunteer a boost! Tell the volunteer how excited you are, say thank you, and let the volunteer know he or she is going to rock it! Remind the volunteer that you'll be available as backup if needed and that you're happy to step in if he or she feels uncomfortable.
3. Here comes the hard part: let the volunteer take the lead and put on the show! You can introduce the volunteer at the beginning of the program and assist as needed, but let the volunteer shine and only step in when absolutely necessary.
4. When the class is over, help your volunteer clean up and have a conversation about
   - • What went well
   - • What could have gone better
   - • Whether the volunteer enjoyed teaching
   - • Whether the volunteer would like to teach again and, if so, when
5. Schedule a time to have the volunteer come back and teach you their next design and go through their next lesson plan.

Design Your Own Rainbow Loom Video

As I commented earlier, Rainbow Looms are makerspaces in themselves. Add in some equipment your kids can use to photograph or record and post their own Rainbow Loom tutorials, and you've added a tech piece of digital creation, not merely digital consumption, that takes your makerspace to the next level! Depending on how detailed the kids want to get, there may even be writing and sound recording opportunities. They can add stop motion or other animation, create their own background music for their video, and add a high-quality voice-over. The sky really is the limit!

Because this is such an involved project you can do it in multiple sessions or as a drop-in program where your teens and 'tweens have access to your equipment at any time while they are working on their videos. Sometimes this approach works better than trying to herd cats and get everyone in one room at the same time. Kids' schedules are busier than ever these days, and one way libraries can compete is by being flexible. To make this program into multiple programs, simply divide up the steps as you see fit or let the kids work at their own pace under your guidance.

Tab Indicators

STEAM

- S: Experimenting with video creation
- T: Producing and promoting videos, doing online research for designs and patterns, using 3D printing for C-clips, hooks, and new types of looms
- E: Filming, creating voice-over, creating music for video, making objects by hand
- A: Designing, being creative, creating nontraditional items with looms (e.g., rugs, yarn bombing), writing scripts, drawing a storyboard
- M: Following patterns, counting, designing patterns

Time

1 or more hours (based on the chosen design and how many sessions you schedule)

Age level

8 to 18 years old

Ingredients

- Flip cams, laptops with cameras and microphones, smart phones, or another recording device with the ability to post to the Internet quickly and easily
- All your Rainbow Loom supplies
- Paper
- Pens/pencils
- Movie-editing software (Don't get crazy unless you want to; Movie Maker or iMovie will work just fine!)

Setup

This will vary depending on what your space is like and how many 'tweens and teens you want participating at one time. But here's a good place to start:

1. Set up at least one table with chairs around it for the discussion portion.
2. Project the YouTube video tutorial examples you've chosen to the group using whatever projection setup you have.
3. Have pens and paper ready for your 'tweens and teens to take notes on what they like and don't like, to write down their standards, and to draw their storyboards.

Instructions

1. Do a little research about what makes a good tutorial. Have examples to show the teens (see the Resources List for some ideas) and ask questions:
   - Do you like the videos where you can see the people in their entirety making the bracelets or do you like it when you can only see their hands? Why?
   - What makes a tutorial clear? Close-ups? Camera focus? Simple instructions spoken while the teacher performs the action? Text with the images?
   - What backdrops look best? Someone standing in the kitchen? Someone hanging out on his or her bed? Using a carpet to create on—or a table?
   - What makes video instructors sound good or bad? How many times do they say "ummm" or "like"? Do they look and sound confident?
   - How long should a video be? Would you rather watch a short video or a longer video? Does the difficulty of your design mean you need a longer video?
   - Taking it even further: What makes a good YouTube video? Humor? Cartoons? Cats? Crazy songs? Can you (and should you) add those elements to what you're doing in your tutorial video?
2. Have participants create a wish list of the standards they want for their video and have them sort them into four categories:
   - The LOOK of the video
   - The SOUND of the video
   - The QUALITY of the video
   - The EXPLANATION of the video
3. Now it's time to make a storyboard! A storyboard is a visual representation of the story you want to tell. You create what looks like a

comic strip that lays out the order of events and important points of your story. The storyboard creates a plan for you to follow when filming and gets you thinking about the look of your video before you start shooting. Explain the concept to the kids and let them start creating. Go around the room and give pointers. Remind the kids to stay true to their video standards.

4. Once the storyboards are complete, let the recording begin! Encourage the group to have fun but stay focused on their standards. They can reshoot if necessary.

Resources

Tutorial video examples:

Official Rainbow Loom instructional videos: https://www.rainbow loom.com/instructions/rainbowloom?field_instruction_level _category_tid=5
How to make a rose ring: https://www.youtube.com/watch?v =zWHjlA_TDrY
How to make a snake charm: https://www.youtube.com/watch?v =tSxOuPCHh0w

Articles:

Scholastic article: What Are Storyboards?: http://www.scholastic .com/teachers/article/what-are-storyboards
Entrepreneur article: "Inventor of the Wildly Popular 'Rainbow Loom' Weaves the American Dream With Rubber Bands in a Detroit Basement": http://www.entrepreneur.com/article/228081
School Library Journal article from the blog A Chair a Fireplace and a Tea Cozy: "Rainbow Bracelets": http://blogs.slj.com/teacozy/ 2013/10/28/rainbow-bracelets/
The Library Voice blog post: "And Just How Does Rainbow Loom Fit Into the Library and School": http://vanmeterlibraryvoice.blog spot.com/2014/01/and-just-how-does-rainbow-loom-fit-into.html

Tips and Tricks

- Metal hooks versus plastic hooks
  - If you have one of the original Rainbow Loom kits then you have plastic hooks. This is fine for basic designs, but as people have been more creative and made designs that involve a lot of doubling, tripling, or quadrupling of bands those plastic hooks can

sometimes fall victim to the strain of tension. Newer kits come with a metal hook, or upgrade kits can be purchased directly from the Rainbow Loom website; these include metal hooks in three different colors. You can also use a crochet hook if you like; any of the smaller sizes (2.75 mm to 3.5 mm) will work great!

- Is it really such a big mistake to buy a knockoff loom brand?
  - I've only played briefly with one particular knockoff loom, but from what I've read and heard there are times the more advanced designs won't work on those looms because
    - They don't have pegs that move, limiting your design options.
    - They can't be combined with other looms, limiting your design options.
    - The pegs are made from a more fragile plastic, so some of the designs that triple or quadruple the bands may break the pegs.

    It seems a wise investment to spend a few extra dollars to avoid these frustrations, and it's nice for the kids to have the top-of-the-line equipment in an arena that won't break your budget.
  - The bands too are available at different quality levels. As I've experimented with the cheaper knockoff brands, I've learned that they stretch differently and maintain elasticity differently over time. In addition, the cheaper bands seem to come in different sizes, even within individual baggies, creating less than perfect designs in the end. My solution is to use the cheaper bands for antiprogramming or day-to-day Rainbow Loom use but to spend the extra money on the higher-quality bands for special projects or programs.

3

◇ ◇ ◇

DISGUSTING SCIENCE

Gross stuff is like 'tween and teen catnip. They flock to it, it revs up their energy, and everyone gets a case of the giggles! Lucky for us nature—and especially the human body—is rife with disgusting stuff and is an easy lesson in STEAM topics!

One of the great things about programs with yuck appeal is that they will generate interest: interest in learning more and interest in the programming you offer. These programs can be run separately or you can make a three-week series out of them.

Not only are disgusting conversations and experiments a lot of fun with this age group but it's also a fantastic way to show off your nonfiction collection and various online databases! Giving 'tweens and teens a peek at how easy the databases are to use and the vast amount of information that lies within will help with their school assignments. Giving them some cool, disgusting books to take home with them will allow them to explore topics even further.

STOCKING THE PANTRY

Most of what you need you already have: paper, space to run around in, etc. However, there are some special things for each program in this chapter that you might not have already. Everything you need is laid out under the Ingredients sections for each program.

PROMOTING YOUR PROGRAM

Spreading the word for a program that is gross will be easy. Kids want the ick factor and will be thrilled you're willing to give them some disgusting, messy fun.

Create a colorful, flashy poster that shows off all the grossness of whichever program you choose, and be sure to talk it up in advance. Word of mouth truly is the best publicity! One idea is to host a whole series of yucky programming for October because that's such a popular time for an ick-fest!

RECIPES

The Disgusting Human Body

If you don't know where to start with disgusting science, this is your winner. Instant gross-out factor, a hook that will draw kids back in the next week, and use of real equipment like in the movies makes for a sure-fire success!

Tab Indicators

STEAM

S: Studying the human body, discussing cleanliness, viewing bacteria, forming a hypothesis on bacteria and molds
T: Using lab equipment: swabs, petri dishes
E: Taking body samples
A: Drawing mold hypothesis
M: Calculating growth of mold

Time

1 hour

Age level

8 to 13 or 14 to 18 years

Ingredients

- Chairs (one per participant)
- 3 or 4 tables to work at (groups of 3 or 4 kids will be at each table)
- Disgusting Science Kit from Fat Brain Toys: http://www.fatbrain toys.com/toy_companies/poof_slinky_inc/scientific_explorer_dis gusting_science.cfm

- A safe place to keep your experiments while they age
- Paper plates you can write on
- Projector
- Projector screen
- Laptop with access to the Internet
- Scrap paper
- Crayons, colored pencils, or markers
- Hand sanitizer
- Trash can

Setup

1. It's a good idea to create the sugar solution for your petri dishes a day or two in advance. Be sure to read the instructions when your kit arrives so you can be ready when the big, disgusting day comes!
2. Prepare your staff to hear a lot of groans, moans, and shrieks of "eeeeew!"
3. Have materials ready to be handed out—but not on tables—to ensure that you keep their attention at the beginning when you'll show photos and encourage discussion.
4. The room should have the tables arranged so that everyone can see you. A horseshoe or arch shape with chairs all on the opposite side of where you'll be speaking is ideal.

Instructions

1. *Discuss cleanliness*: Have your group start off by talking about why it's important to be clean. Reference famous occurrences in history of plagues that were brought on by a lack of cleanliness. For instance, ask kids if they've heard of the Black Death? (Chances are they have.) Ask them if they know what the Black Death actually was? (Chances are they don't.) Blow their little minds by telling them the Black Death was actually something called the bubonic plague, a disease that got its name because of the red spots a person would break out in that eventually turned to black boils the size of eggs or apples that oozed blood and pus. In the Resources section there are links and books with more information on the bubonic plague you can research yourself or share with your kids. The bubonic plague bacteria is carried in the blood of rats. The rats had fleas that bit them. The rats became immune to the plague but the fleas that bit them then bit people and BOOM! Over 20 million people died in just five years.
2. *Discuss what makes you sick*: Take a look at some bacteria, germs, and parasites up close. Use the books you have in your collection as well as a laptop open to an image search using the search engine of

your choice. It's fine to do some research on the really funky looking ones you find to share with your kids, but don't forget about
the standard illnesses they'll know and can be quite interesting
visually, like the flu (influenza), ear infections (bacterium *Moraxella
catarrhalis*), or the bubonic plague referenced earlier.

This is a great opportunity to show off the databases you subscribe to. Get some
amazing high-quality and colorful gross images and drop in a quick plug for the services you offer!

3. *Shout it out*: Have kids yell out gross body parts and what's gross
   about them. Be ready for some giggles over poop, boogers, farts,
   pee, puke, spit, sweat, earwax, and more.
4. *Discuss how dirty the human body is*: Now show some photos of the
   amazing bacteria and germs that live on the human body all the
   time! Again, use a mix of your books and online database images.
   Some sweet spots to look into include our guts (*Clostridium* bacteria), our scalps (lice), our tongues (far too many to list but all are
   really beautiful and living in harmony!), and our skin (methicil-
   lin-resistant *Staphylococcus aureus*, bedbugs, ticks). Eeew!
5. *Explain the instructions of the experiment*: Together, you're going to
   take a close look at the bacteria that live on your body. You'll break
   into teams of three, choose a body part to swab, and then rub your
   swab onto the petri dish. In a week you'll meet again to look at
   how, when well fed, the bacteria grow and can be observed by
   the human eye without a microscope. This is also a helpful time
   to discuss what a hypothesis is. When talking to kids I like to
   describe a hypothesis as an educated guess about what's going to
   happen.
6. *Explain how a petri dish works*: I love Steve Spangler's explanation of
   how this works. (Check out the Resources for a link.) Not only does
   it cover the basics in language kids will understand but it's also a
   great recipe for re-creating this experiment after you've used up
   the ingredients in your Disgusting Science Kit. You'll want to cover
   what solution the bacteria will be living on and eating and how a
   warm, dark place helps them breed.
7. *Give teams their petri dishes and plates*: Have each team member label
   the edge of the plate with his or her name and the gross body part
   they'll be swabbing.
8. *Swab!* Have kids choose an appropriate gross body part and then
   swab it with the cotton swab. Then they can gently smear their
   sample onto the petri dish's sugar solution.
9. *Reiterate*: Explain once more what will happen inside the petri dish
   over the course of the next week.

10. *Hypothesize*: Have kids draw their petri dishes complete and add a hypothesis of what they think their mold will look like next week. Make sure they label it with their name.
11. *Explain yourself*: If you have time, have the kids explain why they drew what they drew. Encourage them to explain the WHY of what they drew and not just fire off a description of what they drew.
12. *Rope 'em in*! Remind kids to come back next week to see their petri dish's progress. Also, this is a great way to lure them back for a new disgusting science program!

Resources

Web resources:

The History Channel's write up of the Black Death (with a great video!): http://www.history.com/topics/black-death
Steve Spangler on growing bacteria in petri dishes: http://www.stevespanglerscience.com/lab/experiments/growing-bacteria

Great books about disgusting diseases:

American Plague: The True and Terrifying Story of the Yellow Fever Epidemic of 1793 by Jim Murphy (ISBN 0395776082)
Fever 1793 by Laurie Halse Anderson (ISBN 0689848919)
How They Croaked: The Awful Ends of the Awfully Famous by Georgia Bragg (ISBN 0802798179)
Oh. Rats! The Story of Rats and People by Albert Marrin (ISBN 0525477624)
Red Madness: How a Medical Mystery Changed What We Eat by Gail Jarrow (ISBN 1590787323)

Recreate a Human Stomach

This program is funny. Sometimes because kids figure out what they're doing right away, and others don't realize what the end product will be until they get there. Either way, it's a great time filled with boisterous squeals of disgust and plenty of poop jokes.

Tab Indicators

STEAM

S: Studying the human body, learning about the gastrointestinal process, learning about muscles, hypothesizing the order of the digestive organs

T: Using measuring equipment
E: Building a human stomach, physically recreating the digestion process
A:
M: Measuring liquids

Time

1 hour

Age level

8 to 13 or 14 to 18 years

Ingredients

- Room to make a mess in; tile floor makes for easier cleanup if you've got it
- Chairs (one per participant)
- Tables to work on
- Balloons (one per person or one per team of two people)
- Plates to work over and catch spills and messes
- One or two slices of whole-grain bread per balloon—the good kind with the seeds and grains you can see all over and through it
- 1 tsp of vinegar per balloon
- 1 Tbsp of oil per balloon
- Trash can
- Small cups (two per balloon)
- Tablespoon and teaspoon measuring spoons (one per balloon)
- Funnels (one per balloon)
- Paper towels
- Spray cleaner that will clean up spilled cooking oil

Setup

1. Have all the materials in the Ingredients section ready to be passed out.
2. If you have the time and resources, pour a little oil into a cup and a little vinegar into a cup for each participant or team.
3. Have these small cups ready to be passed out but not on the tables when they arrive.
4. Set up each participant (or team) with the following: a plate, a teaspoon and a tablespoon measuring spoon, a funnel.
5. Have the balloons ready to go, but unless you're ready to compete with squealing and/or farting balloon noises while you explain what you're doing today I'd suggest holding off on handing them out ahead of time.
6. Set up a trash can or two nearby for kids to dump out their messy experiments when they're all through.

Instructions

1. *Intro to the gastrointestinal (GI) system*: Ask how many organs are used in the digestive process (answer: seven—the esophagus, stomach, pancreas, liver, gallbladder, small intestine, and large intestine). Ask if the kids can put the organs used in the GI system in order correctly (Use the GI System Organ Labels sheet provided in the Resources section!)
2. *Discuss cool digestive facts*:
   a. Cows, formerly thought to have five stomachs, actually have one stomach with four compartments: the rumen and reticulum are where partially chewed food travels and is stored after the cow swallows. After resting, the cow coughs up this undigested food (called cud), chews it better, and swallows it again. Then it travels to the omasum and abomasum where the food is fully digested. For more information and some really cool disgusting images check out the FDA's explanation of a cow's digestive system in Resources.
   b. Carnivorous plants, like the Venus flytrap and pitcher plant don't actually attack and chew their food. They have a sweet-smelling liquid inside them that lures insects in and then eats them slowly because of digestive enzymes it contains. For more information or images on carnivorous plants, take a look at the *Encyclopaedia Britannica* write-up in Resources.
3. *Hand out balloons*: Tell your kids that the balloons will be their stomachs for this experiment. The large balloon shape will be the stomach and the skinny part of the balloon will be the esophagus.
4. *Hand out saliva*: Pass out your cups of oil and let the kids know that this will act as the saliva of your digestive system, coating the walls of your balloon esophagus so the food can easily slide down into the stomach.
5. *Spoon saliva*: Using their funnels and teaspoon have the kids pour their oil into their balloon stomach and coat the interior.
6. *Hand out acid*: Pass out the vinegar and explain how digestive juices break the food down inside your organs.
7. *Spoon acid*: Using their funnels and tablespoons have the kids spoon the acid into their stomachs. At this stage there will probably be some exclamations over the smell coming out of the balloons. It's gross! Be ready for shrieks, screams, gasps, and fake vomiting noises.
8. *Hand out food*: Pass out a piece of bread to each kid or team.
9. *Get chewing*: Explain that in this experiment their hands will be their mouth and tearing the bread up will act as "chewing." Then have the kids tear up their bread!

If you notice the kids tear the bread up quickly into large pieces, let it be. Don't try to get them to tear the bread into smaller pieces. It's a great lesson on chewing your food well when they later try to "swallow" the bread and the pieces are too big. If you get really lucky you'll see some of those large chunks at the end and can really drive the point home!

10. *Eat up*: Time to eat! Have the kids feed their torn-up pieces of bread down the "neck" of the balloon and into their stomachs. This should take time as it's harder than it sounds—even WITH the neck lubricated with oil!

You can decide whether or not folks can team up. It helps to have one person hold open the end of the balloon and another feed the chunks of bread down. This is where having a team makes it easier than going it alone.

11. *Digestion time*: Have the kids mash up the bread once it's all inside the stomach. This will be messy! They may forget to hold their esophagi closed and spill out oil and vinegar. (Hopefully the plates will catch most of the mess, but be ready for some spillage!) While the kids are digesting their food explain that the digestive process takes 12 to 24 hours to complete. Tell them they need to digest their food for at least five minutes before moving on to the next step.

12. *The really gross part*: Now that their food is all digested, their stomachs need to get rid of it to let the small intestine absorb its nutrients. You know what that means: they'll need to push the food through and out their intestines (the neck of the balloon again!). While they're doing this—and before they realize what end product they're creating—you may have time to describe how their intestines use smooth muscles to push the food along its merry way. Smooth muscles are involuntary muscles, meaning you don't have conscious control over them. Be prepared for more shrieks of ickiness and revelry as they realize that what they've been working toward creating this entire time is actually poop.

Don't tell the kids they're making poop. It's way more fun when they realize it for themselves!

Remember earlier when I mentioned that it's not always a bad thing to let the stomachs "eat" pieces of bread that are too big? Have your kids hunt for pieces that were so large they didn't get fully digested, including those hearty grains and seeds in the bread. Point out that they may want to spend a little extra time chewing their food so as to absorb more nutrients in the future!

13. *Clean up*: Now that the digestive process is complete, it's time to throw away this stinky mess! Have kids dump as much of their mess as possible into the trash can you provided, but be ready to do a little extra cleanup with paper towels and spray cleaner.

Resources

Web resources:

Encyclopaedia Britannica's write-up on the GI system (with a short video!): http://www.britannica.com/EBchecked/topic/1081754/human-digestive-system/45317/Esophagus

The University of Missouri's Body Walk program has a great worksheet on the small intestine and digestive science to incorporate into the discussion and generate critical thinking: http://extension.missouri.edu/hesfn/bodywalk/classroom/smallintestine.pdf

"How Cows Eat Grass" by Adam I. Orr is is FDA's explanation of the digestive system of a cow: http://www.fda.gov/AnimalVeterinary/ResourcesforYou/AnimalHealthLiteracy/ucm255500.htm

Encyclopaedia Britannica article on carnivorous plants: http://www.britannica.com/EBchecked/topic/96390/carnivorous-plant

Great books about digestion:

It's Disgusting and We Ate It! True Food Facts from Around the World and Throughout History by James Solheim (ISBN 0689843933)

The Truth About Poop by Susan E. Goodman (ISBN 162765545X)

GI System Organ Labels Sheet

Esophagus   1

Stomach   2

Pancreas   3

Liver   4

Gallbladder   5

Small Intestine   6

Large Intestine
                             7

The Science behind Vampires

This is the perfect program for Halloween or the inevitable rise of a new vampire phenomenon. It has an immaculate blend of ickiness, humor, and running around.

This program is best presented to either teens or 'tweens—however you see fit to break up those age groups. There are visual elements some may find disturbing, including a forensic scientist examining corpses in the documentary segment that explains the science. This will be a draw for some of your 'tweens and teens but may deter others. Be upfront about the ick factor before you begin so no one gets upset.

Tab Indicators

STEAM

S: Hypothesizing about causes of vampire symptoms, learning true causes of vampire symptoms, learning about the decomposition process

T:

E:

A: learning the world history of vampire legends, exploring the story of the real Dracula, viewing documentary segments, learning the history behind Bram Stoker's *Dracula* novel

M:

Time

1 hour

Age level

8 to 14 years

Ingredients

- Symptoms and causes tags (see the Resources list)
- Large paper (Those oversized Post-Its that stick to the wall are great, but butcher paper taped to the wall is cheaper)
- Markers
- Tape
- Projector
- Wall or screen to watch documentary clips
- Internet access to view vampire documentary clips
- Small prizes to give winning team (coupons for free materials, fine forgiveness, etc.)

Setup

1. Tape your large sheet of paper to the wall to take notes on.
2. Tape up two more large sheets on either side of this sheet. Label them "Team 1" and "Team 2."
3. Set up your markers near the paper to take the notes with.
4. Cut out and prepare vampire symptoms labels and vampire causes labels.
5. Tape symptoms and causes up in a general area near the Team 1 and Team 2 papers on the wall so your kids can grab one and place it on their paper easily.
6. Watch the video clips you'll be showing the kids so you know their content and timing.

Instructions

1. *Rumors and accusations*: Ask your kids what they know about vampires and take notes on your large paper. Most likely they'll shout out things like "They have fangs!"; "They turn into bats!"; or "They're super handsome and sparkle in the sunlight!" Your notes don't need to be super specific; just capture the basics (fangs, turn into bats, etc.).
2. *Ancient myth*: Ask them how old the vampire myth is and jot down those answers, too. The answer will probably shock them. The vampire myth did not originate in Transylvania or even with Bram Stoker's famous novel but 4,000 years ago in ancient Mesopotamia with the legend of Lamashtu, the daughter of a sky god with the wings and talons of a bird and sometimes the head of a lioness. She would steal and kill babies, suck the blood of men, and generally wreak havoc. Hers is the oldest recorded story with vampire qualities—the sucking of blood. Many similar stories occur across cultures. In China there were creatures called kuei—reanimated corpses trapped on Earth because of past bad deeds who would rise at night and attack the living. Greek mythology mentions one of Zeus's mortal lovers, Lamia, who was driven mad by Zeus's wife, Hera, when she discovered their affair. Lamia ate all her children, and when she realized what she had done, she became a monster sucking the blood from babies, jealous of their mothers. These myths were carried all across the world by nomadic peoples who would share stories, causing the myths to blend together into common vampire mythologies.
3. *Modern vampires*: Eventually, in the Dark Ages of medieval Europe a vampire frenzy broke out. (Show the Hungarian vampire story from the History Channel at marker 30:20). These kinds of tales were spread for years throughout Europe and were used in some research

by an author who created what would become the most famous vampire story of all.

4. *Dracula*: In 1897 Bram Stoker's famous novel *Dracula* was published. But Stoker was an Irish author who had never even been to Transylvania! Though controversy surrounds Stoker's influence for Count Dracula, we do know that he studied European folklore for years leading up to writing the novel. Most people believe Count Dracula was actually based on a real-life person. Vlad Dracula was a Romanian prince in the 1400s. "Dracula" translates to "son of the dragon," a fitting name for the man also known as Vlad the Impaler. Vlad was a Christian crusader in his day, trying to keep the Turkish Muslims out of his country and kingdom. He earned the nickname "Impaler" for the fields of spikes he kept around his palace. He was quick to kill traitors and enemies by impaling them and leaving them up on these spikes. There are even tales of him dining on elaborate feasts out in the fields of the dead. (Show the video clip from the History Channel documentary about Vlad at marker 13:45).

5. *Symptoms & Causes*: People were looking for answers but falling prey to superstition and fear back then. What could really have been going on? Divide participants into two teams to play Symptoms & Causes. Here are the rules:

   a. Teams take turns choosing a symptom for the other team to determine a scientific cause for.

   b. Teams win points by pairing the correct scientific cause with the correct vampirism symptom.

      i.   If they get it right the first time they get 10 points.

      ii. If they change their answer to the correct answer they get 5 points.

      iii. If they have the correct answer and change to an incorrect answer they get 0 points.

      iv. If they have an incorrect answer and change to another incorrect answer they get 0 points.

   c. The first team who can tell you what Dracula means gets to start the game!

   d. Play until each side has gone through all symptoms.

6. *What's really going on*? Time for the big reveal! Watch the History Channel documentary segment on the vampire legend of James Spalding at marker 7:19. After it plays ask the team with the symptom "vampires rising from their graves" if their answer is correct or if they would like to change their answer. If they have the answer correct and stick with it they get 2 points. If they change their answer to the correct answer they get 1 point. If they change their answer and it's incorrect they get 0 points. Watch the Live Science video on vampire history and pellagra. Afterward, ask the team with the symptoms of

"drinking blood" and "fear of sunlight" if their answers are correct. Watch the History Channel Documentary segment labeled "The Science" at marker 41:53 and then address the remaining symptoms. The winning team gets whatever prize you like—extra 3D printing time, free movie rentals, fine forgiveness—whatever floats your boat!

7. *Farts: The be all and end all of vampires*: To me, it's hilarious that most of the symptoms of vampirism can be chalked up to corpses simply having gas. Play this up with your group on their way out to get everybody laughing.

Resources

Web resources:

"Vampires: Fact, Fiction, and Folklore by Benjamin Radford," a Live Science article on vampire history with great video (that's less than two minutes!) explaining pellagra, a vitamin deficiency with symptoms similar to the symptoms of vampirism: http://www.live science.com/24374-vampires-real-history.html

"How Vampires Work" by Tom Harris: http://science.howstuffworks .com/science-vs-myth/strange-creatures/vampire1.htm

Encyclopaedia Britannica article on Vlad the Impaler by Richard Pallardy: http://www.britannica.com/EBchecked/topic/631524 /Vlad-III

History Channel Documentary: *Vampire Secrets* (2006), produced by Indigo Films: http://documentaryaddict.com/Vampire+Secrets -1096-doc.html

    7:19–10:19: James Spalding (3 minutes)
    13:45–15:35: Vlad Dracula story (1 minute, 50 seconds)
    30:20–37:47: Hungarian vampire story (8 minutes, 7 seconds)
    41:53–44:32: The Science! (2 minutes, 39 seconds)

Fun books:

How They Croaked: The Awful Ends of the Awfully Famous by Georgia Bragg (ISBN 0802798179)

Vampireology: The True History of the Fallen Ones by Archer Brookes, Nick Holt, and others (ISBN 0763649147)

Vlad the Impaler: The Real Count Dracula by Enid A. Goldberg (ISBN 0531138984)

Symptoms & Causes Sheet

Cut these out and get them ready to be taped onto your Team 1 and Team 2 sheets of paper. (Pssst! Both symptoms and causes are listed in matching order!) The extra causes are to throw your kids off, but don't tell them that!

Symptoms

Vampires rising from their graves

Walking around at night incoherently

Appearance of a beard (hair growing)

Long nails

"Blood" seeping from mouth

Well-fed-looking bodies on corpses that were thin when buried

Moving corpse

Groaning corpse

Fear of sunlight

Drinking blood

Causes

People buried alive

Insomnia

Dehydration pulls back skin, revealing stubbly beard

Dehydration pulls back skin, revealing longer looking nails

Red decompositional fluids building up in the body
push out gases

Bloating due to gases building up

Gasses build up and as they release can make a corpse move

Release of gases causes vocal sounds or gurgling
from the corpse

Vitamin deficiency

Vitamin deficiency

Cursed by a dark entity

Driven mad by Hera, Zeus's wife

Bitten by vampire bat

Farts

Hanging out with a bad crowd

Tips and Tricks

- The Disgusting Science Kit includes other projects that you can easily use for more gross science programs. Explore them with your kids, find out what they want, and then give it to them!
- Maybe you noticed I broke this program into distinct 'tween and teen age groups. This is very intentional. While both age groups may want to participate, their senses of humor revolving around gross subjects are developmentally very different. You want your 'tweens to be unabashedly giggly and innocent when it comes to these activities. You want them erupting in hysterics at the mention of the words bowels, back end, fart, and poop. If they're mixed up with teenagers they may feel too self-conscious to really let themselves go and enjoy the silliness. Similarly, teens may let a particular four letter s-word slip out or tell jokes that are inappropriate for a 'tween to hear. Don't rob them of the chance to explore this disgusting area in their own developmentally appropriate way either.
- The s-word. When I just mentioned it you may have tensed up and decided on the spot to NEVER RUN ANY OF THESE PROGRAMS. That's your choice, and I totally get not wanting to be put in the position to have to kick anyone out, let alone creating the very program that leads to a word that might get them kicked out. However, teens especially are experimenting with language, and if your program is viewed as a safe place where they can let a little potty talk slip, then show them how cool you are by addressing it but letting it slide. Just this once. Also, they may die laughing if you repeat the word back to them instead of calling it the s-word. Just sayin'.

In the next chapter we'll step up your crafting game with some cool tech crafting alternatives that will wow the kids. Even if you're not electronically gifted (like me) you can make these work and further intrigue your kids with the potential for their own artistic abilities!

4

◆ ◆ ◆

DIY MODERN CRAFTS

The maker movement that is sweeping the world is an incredible way to get kids experiencing new projects and potential passions! Across the globe, classrooms, museums, and libraries are all reimagining their spaces to offer more opportunities for families to tinker, create, engineer, and craft within. In this chapter you'll try two different takes on technology. The first is an excellent beginner's take on wearable electronics. The simple method can be adapted for many projects. The second is a hands-on project that takes time and is an anti-tech appreciation of one of the hottest games around—Minecraft.

These projects are perfect for grant writing, so if you have a grant application coming up and you've been struggling with what to ask for—look no further!

STOCKING THE PANTRY

Sites like sparkfun.com and Adafruit.com are fabulous for having high-quality versions of the equipment you need AND offering helpful tutorials. Many big-box stores don't carry equipment like LED lights, conductive thread, or sewable battery holders. You're more likely to have luck finding things like needle-nose pliers, batteries, alligator clips, heat shrink and nail polish at those stores. Of course you'll want to shop around for the best prices possible, but as a starting point you can't go wrong with their kits.

PROMOTING YOUR PROGRAM

Using some of these projects will definitely get people talking about your cool blending of crafts and tech. There's nothing like actually showing off the amazing item to get teens and 'tweens interested in creating their own! Your cyborg pinup flower is a natural accessory to wear leading up to Halloween and through the holidays.

Your sweet new creeper cup can be your water glass at work; it sends out the signal that you are a Minecraft-friendly establishment! Be ready to talk a LOT of Minecraft once you bust it out. If you aren't familiar yet, there are books available in the Resources section about that program, or you can peek here: http://minecraft.gamepedia.com/Minecraft_Wiki.

A poster with some blinking LEDs will always catch some attention, too, and once you know how to do the first project you can go to town hooking up LEDs on everything—your posters, your coworkers, your cat . . .

RECIPES

Cyborg Pinup Flowers and Cyborg Feltie Pins

If you're nervous about getting into electronics then this is the project for you: instant gratification, no soldering, and a simple design that will leave you looking like a genius! It's an ideal taste of what's possible with electronics, especially wearable electronics. It can inspire your teens to explore electronics projects on their own and will open new doors for you by dipping your toes in a manageable electronics program.

Once you've completed a test run of this project, do a little research on potential electronics programs you would consider running in the future. You can crowd-source at the end of the program to find out what's most appealing to your audience and give them ownership over the programming direction of the library!

In addition to this project think about the different ways you can adapt this information into new projects, like making plushies with light-up eyes, bike accessories, wrist bands, and (to keep your parents happy) customized Halloween safety blinkers that aren't lame.

You'll definitely want to test this project out before you teach it if you're new to electronics or to wearable electronics. Not only will you be well versed in the process but you'll also have one to wear around and help promote your program! Once you've created one of these bad boys consider the amount of attention you'll need to give your 'tweens and teens as they create their own and plan for a number of kids that works for you. If you already know you'd like to do more projects like this one, now's the time to think up a couple of examples to run by your kids.

Tab Indicators

STEAM

S: Learning about electric circuits, testing battery leads
T: Using electrical equipment, using sewing equipment
E: Creating an electrical circuit, sewing by hand, using tools
A: Creatively modifying a flower
M: Measuring heat shrink

Time

1 hour

Age level

8 to 18 years

Ingredients

- Two-ply conductive thread: https://www.adafruit.com/products/640
- Sewable CR2032 coin cell battery holders: https://www.sparkfun.com/products/8822
- CR2032 lithium coin cell batteries: http://www.flashingblinkylights.com/light-up-products/wholesale-bulk-batteries/cr2032-batteries.html

- Gold eye embroidery needles: http://www.joann.com/clover-gold -eye-embroidery-needle/1074541.html#q=gold+eye+needle&start=1
- Nail polish (whatever you have lying around will do the trick, but clear is the best)
- Three-mm bare LED lights: http://www.adafruit.com/category/37
- Heat shrink: https://www.adafruit.com/products/1649
- Flower hair clips: http://www.orientaltrading.com/fiesta-flower -hair-clips-a2-14_471.fltr?Ntt=hair%20flower
- Needle-nose pliers
- Alligator clip test leads
- Hair dryer or heat gun
- Felt (multiple colors to choose from)
- Markers
- Scissors
- Rulers

Setup

1. Set up tables and chairs for participants. Each person will need a desk's worth of space to tinker in.
2. The following can be evenly spread out among the tables: heat shrink, scissors, markers, rulers, nail polish, and a spool of conductive thread per table.
3. Each participant's spot should have the following: pliers, battery, battery holder, hair flower, scissors, needle.
4. In a final area, set up the heat gun or hair dryer—away from all the small pieces you've got scattered about. You don't want them blowing away!

Instructions

1. Before creating this fun little accessory it helps to understand how an electrical current works. (Both for you AND your kids!) To make a lightbulb shine you need to provide it with power and it needs to complete an electrical circuit that leads back to that power source.
   a. For this project electrical power comes from the battery.
   b. The battery has a positive and a negative side, just like your LED lights.
   c. For the energy to flow through the circuit you need to attach positive ends to positive ends and negative ends to negative ends.
   d. The conductive thread is made of metal, which will carry the power from the battery to the LED light and then back to the battery, completing the circuit and letting your LED shine!

2. Now that you know how your creation will work you can get started! Test your LEDs on your battery to figure out which is the positive end and which is the negative end. Your battery is marked with - and + symbols. When your LED lights up, whichever prong from your LED is touching the + side of your battery is your positive prong. Mark both your positive prongs with a marker to keep track for later.

3. Cut two pieces of heat shrink about a quarter-inch long.

4. Bend the positive lead of one LED at a 90° angle and then slip one piece of heat shrink over it.

5. Holding the negative lead with your needle-nose pliers, shrink the heat shrink using your heat gun or hair dryer. Using the pliers will help keep your hands out of the way of the very hot air and the metal, which will heat up as the gun does its thing.

6. Once the heat shrink has shrunk and the metal has cooled down, twist together the positive lead of your first LED with the positive lead of your second LED.

7. Repeat steps 4 through 6 for your negative leads.

8. Using your needle-nose pliers, bend both the twisted up positive and negative leads of the LEDs into spirals leaving enough room in their centers to pass a needle and thread through. If you're worried about leaving enough room you could wrap your ends around a pencil, chopstick, or some other common cylindrical item.

9. Congratulations, your LED unit is assembled!

10. Now, take your assembled LED unit and figure out where you want it positioned on your flower.

11. Position your sewable battery holder on the back of the flower behind where you want your LED lights to go.

12. Use your conductive thread to sew the positive end of the battery holder to your flower, leaving a tail so you can tie a knot at the end. Be sure you only sew this one side, as sewing with conductive thread is not like regular sewing! If you keep sewing and attach the negative side too, you will not have an electrical circuit that will work, and your LEDs won't light up. The circuit we're creating is polarized, meaning it can only be connected in one direction. If you were to sew both sides onto your flower with one continuous span of thread you would NOT be completing the circuit in one direction. You'd literally be crossing your wires! The best result is that your flower won't work. The very worst outcome is that you might break some of your pieces.

13. When this first, positive side of your battery holder is sewn to the positive end of your LED unit, tie your two thread ends into a knot and then paint it with the nail polish to hold it together. Conductive thread is thick and prefers to be uncoiled so knots you tie easily

become untied. The nail polish will seal your knot and keep you happy.

14. Repeat steps 12 and 13 with the negative (-) end of your battery.

15. Now for the big test! Insert your battery so that positive sides are touching—and your LEDs should come to life! (If they don't come to life, flip your battery before you disassemble all your hard work to try again.)

16. So you don't kill your favorite new toy, take the battery out when you're not wearing it to preserve its life.

17. Did you find some potential new programs for your new electronics addicts? If so, now is the time to share them or have a vote to determine what project they'd like to do next!

If the flower project is too "girly" for some of your teens, or you'd rather start with a more neutral design, you can create any face out of felt and markers then use the same circuit to make the eyes of your artwork glow. You'll want two pieces of felt so that the circuit lies between them and the battery casing lies on the back piece. Then simply hot-glue a pin back onto the back and you've got a fun, flashy, feltie pin!

These are especially great to create around Halloween for those who plan to do outdoor activities like trick or treating at night. They make kids visible but can be customized to match costumes, a feat no glow stick can accomplish. Score! Here's an example of a light-up skull:

Resources

Web resources:

Super-great explanation of polarity from Sparkfun: https://learn
.sparkfun.com/tutorials/polarity
Helpful article with a simple explanation of how electrical currents
work: Johannes, MD, 2014, "Electricity," *World Book Student,* world
bookonline (subscription required): http://www.worldbookonline
.com/student/article?id=ar177040

These are some great books for reading up more on wearable electronics:

*Make Wearable Electronics: Design, Prototype and Wear Your Own Interac-
tive Garments* by Kate Hartman (ISBN 1449336515)
*Sew Electric: A Collection of DIY Projects That Combine Fabric, Electronics,
and Programming* by Leah Buechley (ISBN 0989795608)

Minecraft Glass Etching

While this program may not be modern in the tech sense that it twinkles
or lights up, it's a perfect crafty activity for a thoroughly popular game
these days. Minecraft is huge. Whether you play it at your library or not,
your fans will love this chance to make an item to keep!

Because of the pixilated nature of the game's artwork, the images transfer well onto two-dimensional surfaces. We'll use a Creeper as an example
for this craft, but your kids may be able to make other designs, too! A
Creeper is a living, moving game entity from Minecraft that tries to get
close to you, the player, so that it can then explode, causing you damage.

This craft is a bit different from many others in that the label on the
bottle states: "Not indicated for use by children." The etching cream eats
away at the surface of the glass and can cause a chemical burn if you get
it on your skin and allow it to sit there. You may consider yourself all
the adult supervision needed, you may want to limit the number of your
participants further than is typical, or you may want to make this a family
program where adults need to be present. It's your call. You know what's
right for your space and your community.

Tab Indicators

STEAM

S: Experimenting with applying cream and tape
T: Using glass-etching equipment,

E: Creating an image using tape, applying etching cream evenly, removing etching cream, cutting tape for design

A: Placing an image on glass, taking artistic license with design

M: Spatially applying tape to create a design, measuring tape for the design

Time

1+ hour

Age level

8 to 18 years

Ingredients

- Any glass without curves or angles. Check your local thrift stores or dollar stores for inexpensive options, but be sure you're buying glass. Glass etching cream will not work on certain types of Pyrex.
- Etching cream, available in a 10-oz. size: http://www.amazon.com /Armour-Etch-15-0200-Cream-10-Ounce/dp/B001BE3UM4
- Masking tape
- Scissors
- Rubber gloves (optional)
- Paintbrushes
- Disposable cups
- Paper towels
- Cleaning spray
- Pencils
- Rulers

If you have a vinyl cutter you can simply cut the images and give your 'tweens and teens a sticker to put on their glass and etch around. This will take considerably less time and will utilize different technology skills in a STEAM sense.

Setup

1. Arrange tables and chairs, leaving enough room for teens to work messily.
2. Each participant's spot should have a glass, a disposable cup, and a paintbrush.
3. Tape, pencils, rulers, and scissors can be spread throughout the work area.
4. You'll want an additional activity for teens to participate in while the etching cream does its thing for at least a half an hour. Antiprogramming stations will do wonders for this, or else you'll need to plan

accordingly. You could release a whole new set of Minecraft books; have a teen give a demonstration on how to create some cool or rare tool; create a Minecraft version of rock, paper, scissors (Creeper, Spider, Water) and have a tournament; show a YouTube video on creating a Minecraft-inspired Rainbow Loom project. Get creative!

Instructions

1. To start out you'll want to set a more serious tone than is typical for most events. Etching cream can burn if it gets on your skin, but that doesn't mean the kids should freak out if that happens. Freaking out could startle others, causing them to accidentally get the cream on themselves. It's important to communicate to your teens that this behavior will result in their needing to leave the program and their work behind since it will create an unsafe work environment for all participants. Instead of freaking out, if they get the cream on themselves they should let you know then head to the restroom and thoroughly wash off whatever area they got the cream on.

2. With that out of the way you can now explain a bit about how etching cream works. Etching cream is a compound that eats away at the smooth surface of glass creating a matte finish and unpolished surface. Wherever they place the etching cream will result in this matte finish.

3. Demonstrate the layout of the Creeper's face, showing which parts are whole strips of tape and which parts are half strips of tape. There is a diagram of the Creeper's face available at the end of this chapter. Luckily, the boxy artwork of Minecraft makes it very easy to transfer into other art forms like this one. Point out that they'll need to measure the width of their tape and then use that as their standard unit of measurement when recreating the Creeper's face. For example, if your masking tape is 1″ wide, each eyeball of the Creeper needs to be a 1″ × 1″ square. If your masking tape is ½″ wide, each eyeball needs to be a ½″ × ½″ square, and so on.

4. Have the kids start cutting and applying their strips of tape accordingly. Make yourself available to answer questions and offer assistance. Pencils and rulers should be available to make more precise measurements.

5. Once they have their tape applied to their glasses have them firmly push down all edges of the tape so no areas of the cream can seep underneath. If cream does get underneath they won't have straight lines but wobbly ones. On the other hand, remind them that this being their first time their designs may not be perfect. This isn't a huge deal since if they like doing this you can offer another class for them to use to improve!

6. Once their edges are firmly secured you can now demonstrate how to apply the etching cream. It's helpful to show that if the cream isn't applied evenly the result will be uneven etching. A thick layer should be applied to ensure even etching and a more uniform look. A quick reminder to stay cool is typically helpful at this point as well.

7. Go around and pour about a half-ounce of etching cream in people's cups and encourage them to get etching!

8. Roam around, keeping an eye on the thickness and uniformity of their etching cream. Let them know if you see a spot that needs a little help.

9. When their designs are done they should just leave them on the table. Have them bring their cup with the remaining cream and paintbrush to you and then go wash their hands thoroughly.

10. You can use the brush to pour the cream back into the bottle and then ditch the cups. The brushes can be rinsed out later.

11. When their hands are washed they can go participate in one of your antiprogramming stations or engage in whatever special treat you've prepared for them.

12. The cream will have done a good job of etching after 30 minutes. At that time you can call them back and have them bring their glasses to the bathroom to rinse off the etching cream and masking tape. Any tape that gets in the sink can be thrown away by the teens. Once they dry their glass they'll really be able to see the effect the cream has had!

13. Once all the glasses are rinsed you can rinse off your paintbrushes and wash down the workspace you used today. Etched glass is a permanent change and can go in the dishwasher. You can feel free to use your glass right away!

Resources

Web resources:

For more information on glass etching: www.etchworld.com
The Official Minecraft Wiki: http://minecraft.gamepedia.com /Minecraft_Wiki

Helpful Minecraft books:

Minecraft: The Complete Handbook Collection by Stephanie Milton, Paul Soares Jr., Jordan Maron, and Nick Farwell (ISBN 0545685192)
Minecraft for Dummies by Jacob Cordeiro (ISBN 1118537149)

Tips and Tricks

- If you'd like to test-run playing with electronics to make sure it's something you're comfortable with, I recommend the beginner LED sewing kit made by Adafruit. It includes snaps, four LED lights, two sewable battery holders, two lithium coin cell batteries, a bobbin of two-ply conductive thread, and a pack of sewing needles: https://www.adafruit.com/products/1285. You'll need to find your own nail polish, tools, and heat shrink, but it's enough equipment to get you up and running and confident in your program.
- When it comes to glass etching you may want to purchase rubber gloves for your teens to wear. In the past, however, when I've tried this they end up fitting poorly, resulting in accidental smears and frustration. In addition, there was a lot of worry about getting the cream on them onto their hands when they were taking them off. Feel free to try the gloves for yourselves and see if your teens have a better experience with them!
- I've run the glass-etching program with 'tweens aged 8 to 12 in the past and have had great results. I recommend getting your feet wet with your teenage group and then branching out with your 'tweens when you've gained some comfort and experience teaching the project.
- If parents are worried about their child participating in a class where the etching cream is used, commend them for being great parents and invite them to come and assist their child so they can both see the careful process you're engaged in and be their child's backup if they feel they need to be.

After the tech focus of this chapter has spawned some interesting discussion among your teens and 'tweens, it's the perfect time to launch into the next chapter, which is on 3D printing. You'll take the tech focus from the realm of physical engineering to science fiction!

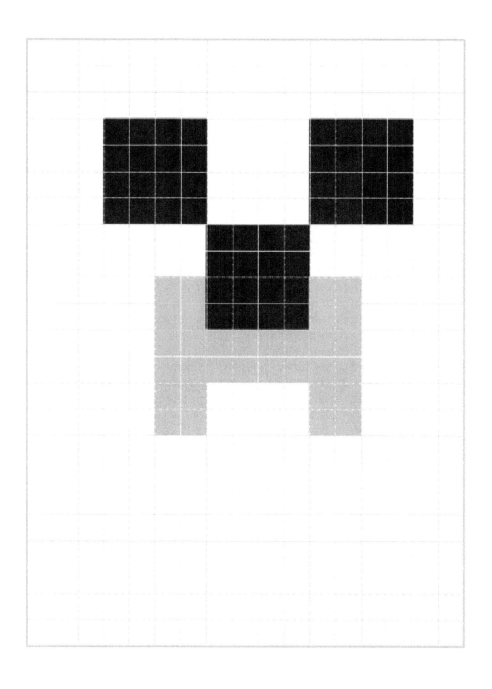

5
◇ ◇ ◇

THE 3 Ds OF 3D PRINTING

No doubt about it, 3D printing is one of the hottest topics in libraries right now. It seems like everyone either already has one or is trying to get one. But the big struggle is what to do with the thing once you've got it. It's a good idea to check one out in action before you buy one, especially if you don't have any tech staff. Call your state library organization to see who may already be using one and then call to schedule a visit in person. You'll want to be sure to ask questions about that library's experience with setup and maintenance and how much time it takes them to explain the process to patrons.

Once a 3D printer is acquired, how do you structure its use so it isn't monopolized by one person? How can you ensure that it is a learning tool and not just a machine kids dictate you to crank out useless garbage on? Scariest of all: How can you ensure that it doesn't become the only part of your job that gets attention while other things fall by the wayside?

This simple program was designed to answer all these questions and to give you a framework to develop your 3D printer into a tool that works for you, not against you! It's written for those using a MakerBot 3D printer and the software that goes with it, but the general ideas can be applied to other 3D printers. Mostly, this is a program that's a guided show-and-tell with you walking the user through the use of a couple pieces of software and making yourself available to answer questions and play tour guide.

You could say that the 3 Ds in 3D printing stand for

- Duplicate
- Design
- Dream big

STOCKING THE PANTRY

Of course, you need a 3D printer, or access to one, but there are a few other appendages you should have as well.

- 3D printer: MakerBot, available here: www.MakerBot.com
- Computer to hook up to the MakerBot
- 3D printer filament
- A Tinkercad account setup: www.tinkercad.com

3D printer filament, a corn-based product, is pretty inexpensive. Rolls of 2.2 lb are available from UltiMachine (www.ultimachine.com), and the cost is just pennies per gram! If you do need to charge your patrons for the filament use to ensure that your 3D printer is a sustainable practice for your library, this means you can do so without breaking the bank. A print of 45 minutes or less typically costs less than a dollar!

You'll want to set up the 3D printer in a prominent place that can handle a little bit of robotic noise as the 3D printer does make some pretty cool whirring noises.

PROMOTING YOUR PROGRAM

A great way to promote your 3D printer is to invite school groups in to get a demonstration. The kids can get a short demo then come back after school to create their own 3D printed object!

Reaching out to the press is another great idea. Tech stuff is always such a hot topic with the media—and people love knowing when their community is in groundbreaking territory!

Ultimately, this thing will advertise itself. When word gets out that you have a 3D printer, people will come by just to see it in action!

RECIPES

Duplicate

Duplicate is the ideal place to start learning about 3D printing. The idea of creating nearly anything you can imagine is overwhelming. Duplicate gives you insight into what others are creating while also teaching the basics of how to download, what type of file to choose, how to open your design in your new software, and then how much time and filament it actually takes to create an object.

Tab Indicators

STEAM

S: Hypothesizing build times, hypothesizing MakerWare program functions

T: Using equipment: 3D printer, Internet, MakerWare program

E: Creating an object using a 3D printer; learning about moving, turning, viewing, and scaling an object in MakerWare

A: Studying objects created using 3D modeling software

M: Estimating the size of an object in relation to amount of time it will take to print, learning about angles on objects and how to support them

Time

20-minute lesson, 30-minute print exercise

Age level

8+ years

Ingredients

- 3D printer
- 3D printer filament
- Computer hooked up to a 3D printer with Internet access and Maker-Ware installed
- Needle-nose pliers
- Putty knife

Setup

1. Have your 3D printer set up and ready to go. Simply follow the instructions that come with it.
2. Have MakerWare installed on the computer you'll be using with the 3D printer. Again, just follow the instructions. It's easy!
3. Give this stage a try on your own—it's a great learning tool and will give you experience you can relate to your kids, 'tweens, and teens!
4. Create a few objects printed within different time frames (an object that took 15 minutes to print, 30 minutes to print, 45 minutes to print, 1 hour to print, 3 hours to print, 10 hours to print, etc.)

Instructions

1. Start off with an explanation. This step of 3D printing is all about learning the basics and what's involved in getting started.
2. Show the preprinted object and have kids guess how long it took to print. Usually kids are surprised by just how long it takes to

print things. Explain that to be fair and give everyone a chance to try the 3D printer, everyone is given a 30-minute print time. Show them your 30-minute print and explain that an object printed in 30 minutes will fit in the palm of their hand.

The 30-minute print time is something we change a lot here in Chattanooga. Initially, we didn't have any time limits; we wanted to see what would happen in this scenario. We found that there would be some kids who simply wanted to print out a little Minion to take home and put in their room but other kids who wanted to make the biggest thing they could find just so they could make the biggest thing they could find. As prints tended to get bigger, people would want to leave and come back later to pick them up, which wasn't a huge deal. Then folks started e-mailing us their designs to print for them to pick up later, which again wasn't a huge deal. However, when we were teaching the lessons, taking e-mail orders, and dealing with no time limits we found that we were outnumbered and overwhelmed. We've played around with different time frames and find that a half an hour is a great amount of time for kids who want to experience the 3D printer and for parents who want them to get that experience but don't want to hang out all day.

3. Open up the www.Thingiverse.com website. Show the kids the front page and teach them how to surf for a design. Some suggested surfs:
   a. Surf through the cool home page where things are always changing and sometimes there are design contests.
   b. Click on the Explore tab and choose Categories from the dropdown menu that appears. This lets you think about the objects in a new way. The toys category will have neat things like Legos, yo-yos, tops, and more. Fashion will have wearable things like necklace pendants or rings. Household will have things for life hacks and stuff for their rooms.
   c. Click on the search window and type in what they're looking for. They can hunt for Minecraft, Hello Kitty, Zelda, whatever!
4. Show them that there will be some designs (like wristwatches) that have extra parts not created on a 3D printer. The watch has a motor that won't be printed. Similarly, some watch bands will need to be glued together or assembled using extra parts they may not have, like pins. Suggest that for their first print a good choice is an object that will fit in the palm of their hands, is just one piece, and can be printed in whatever color you have hooked up to your machine.
5. When they have a good design, walk them through the various information tabs below the image of the object.
   a. Thing Info offers a brief description of the object and maybe a little about the creator's process in designing the object.

b. Instructions tells you how to assemble the object after it's printed or if the object is more than one color how to print it in the correct color order. (This is a great way to show kids how many pieces an object is really made of. Things that look like one piece may actually be two; it's always a good idea to double-check here before downloading.)

c. Thing Files shows you how many files you'll be downloading (another great way to tell how many pieces an object is) and what kind of file you'll be downloading. MakerBots can only make stereolithography files or .stl files, so this is a great tab to have kids look through to be sure they're downloading an .stl file that will actually print!

d. Comments are where people who have tried to print the object say whether or not it was successful. They also may talk about tweaks they made to the design in another program.

e. Made is just what it sounds like; it tells you how many times this object has been printed. Usually there are also pictures of the made objects in different colors of filament.

f. Collections are folders made by different users of Thingiverse to house similar designs. Clicking Collections shows you the different Collections this object has been added to.

g. Remixes are tweaks and edits that have been made to this object and then posted here for other to see.

When teaching these steps it's important to let your 'tweens and teens "drive" and actually perform these steps. Buzzing through them yourself will get the object printed faster but won't effectively teach them how it's done. Let them stumble a bit finding the buttons and ask if they'd like help before giving it.

6. Have them click Download Now and it will reopen the Thing Files tab you already viewed. Click Download This Thing. The object should now appear in the Prepare window of the MakerWare desktop you installed.

7. A screen may pop up that asks you if you'd like to resize the object so it fits. Always choose this option or you'll get something super small that's really hard to work with or something super huge that's really hard to work with.

8. Another screen that may pop up will ask you if you'd like to move the object to the platform. Always choose to move it to the build platform or it will hover in midair and when you start to print it, you will wind up with tangly strings of nothingness, not the beautiful YOLO keychain this kid had his or her heart set on.

9. Now that your object is sitting pretty on the MakerWare build plate go over the buttons on the side of the screen with them. Have them

guess what they do one by one. The first button (and the one that is already selected when you open the program) is View. By holding down the left mouse button they can spin around their design and look at it from all angles. When they move on to their next button and View is no longer selected, they can still use View by clicking and holding down the right mouse button. (Some kids will know what a right mouse button is and others won't. Be ready to explain!)

10. They'll feel like a big shot (or look at you like you're an idiot) when you tell them to guess what the Move button does. Of course it moves things. However, you must click on the object first to move it around the screen. Explain that the build plate on the screen represents the one inside the 3D printer. Be sure to mention that if they scoot their object half off the build plate and then try to print it, the machine will do its best to give them what they asked for. Dutifully it will stream extra filament all over the place when it gets to the edge, ruining the one good half of their design that it already started on the build plate.

11. Ask them to guess what the next button down—Turn—does. They will also probably get this one right. It spins the object around. Once the button is selected, though, have them hover the mouse over it again. An extra triangle will appear off to the side of the button. When they click on the button again they get a more accurate method for turning their object on three different axes. Let them play around with this for a while, and then show them how to put their object back the way it was.

12. The final button for them to figure out is Scale. Usually this is the tricky one. This button makes the object larger or smaller if you hold down the left mouse button and drag the mouse in and out. This is incredibly exciting to the kids and will certainly generate the most giggles. Let them make their object far too large to ever print and so small they can barely see it. As they're playing, point out that when they click and drag they'll see a white line appear. Following the white line will help them perfect their scaling abilities. Have them hover and click again on the scale button for more precise options to use when scaling their object. Finally, have them guess at how large the object should be to print within the 30-minute time frame.

13. Click on the tab labeled Settings. Explain that printing at different resolutions is like the difference between looking at a picture and a pixilated image. The lower the resolution of the image the greater the pixilation. A pixilated image will print faster and be a bit chunkier looking, just like an object with a lower resolution. An object with a higher resolution will print slowly, but it will come

out looking smoother. Typically, it's a good idea to start with a lower resolution for their first object for more wow factor.

14. Now explain that a raft is a sheet of plastic that prints underneath their design and will protect the object when it's time to take it off the build plate. It's always a good idea to print your objects with a raft. On top of protecting your 3D printed object if it needs to be scraped off the build plate, it's also easier for the filament to stick to the build plate if it starts with the thicker extruded filament used on the bottom of a raft. Without the raft some objects will fare just fine, but occasionally the finer filament used for the actual 3D design won't stick to the build plate and will slide around, sticking instead to your extruder and creating a potential fire hazard.

15. Supports are pieces of thin, snappable plastic that support overhang in your design. A good way to think about it is that anything under a 45-degree angle will not print properly for the same reason we always move the design to the build plate; it won't be touching anything, so it'll just become a stringy, messed ball of filament hanging off the side of your otherwise perfect design. Ugh. Take a look at the design and decide together if it needs supports.

16. Click Print. A new screen will pop up telling you how much filament you will use and how long your print will take.

17. If the object prints within the 30-minute time limit, go ahead and click Start Print! If not, cancel out of these two screens and have them resize the object and try again. (This may take several tries.)

18. Once you've clicked Start Print and things are ready to go, give them a quick tour of your machine. Show them the filament on its spools, explain how it feeds into the small motor and out of the extruder, and look at the information that your display screen will tell them. Have them watch their raft print and the first few layers of their design to be sure you aren't working with a corrupt file or that the machine doesn't need some tweaking. Once it's through those layers and there are no problems they can play with all your other cool stuff.

19. When their design is done, remove it from the build plate for them (you may need to scrape it off with the putty knife) and have them snap off the raft and supports. (They may need the pliers for this part!)

Design

Now that they have an understanding of using MakerWare and how the 3D printing process works they can get creative and make something of their own! Tinkercad is a very easy drag-and-drop type program that provides a good introduction to 3D design.

Tab Indicators

STEAM

S: Hypothesizing build times

T: Using equipment: 3D printer, Internet, MakerWare program, Tinkercad program

E: Creating an object using a 3D printer; moving, turning, viewing, and scaling the object in MakerWare; building a 3D design in Tinkercad

A: Designing an object

M: Estimating the size of an object in relation to amount of time it will take to print, learning about angles on objects and how to support them

Time

20-minute lesson, 30-minute print time

Age level

8+ years

Ingredients

- 3D printer
- Computer hooked up to a 3D printer with Internet access and MakerWare installed
- 3D printer filament

Setup

1. Create an account with www.Tinkercad.com, a free Web-hosted 3D design program.
2. Log in to Tinkercad.
3. Have your 3D printer turned on and ready to go.

Instructions

1. Introduce your teens or 'tweens to Tinkercad. Have them click on the Start Tinkering Now button on the home page.
2. Start by showing them the build plate they'll be creating on. Similar to MakerWare, by holding down the right mouse button and rotating they can change their view of the build plate. If you scroll using the mouse you can zoom in and out.
3. On the right side of the screen is a panel filled with shapes, letters, numbers, designs, and some random chicken and bunny parts. Let

them know that although these pieces are shown in different colors, that's only to make designing easy. When their object prints it will still only be one color.

4. Drag and drop a cube onto the build plate. Show them that when you click on the square you will see multiple black and white squares appear around it. By clicking on the black squares at the base corners of the cube and dragging you can stretch its corners in different directions. By clicking and dragging the white squares on the base sides of the cube you can stretch its sides.

5. There is a black square at the top of your cube that will make it taller or shorter by clicking and dragging.

6. The arrows around the base rotate the cube by clicking and rotating them.

7. There is a cone at the very top of your cube. Clicking this and dragging it lifts your cube off of the build plate. This is great for designing but remind them that their design will have to be touching the build plate to actually print.

8. Drag some more shapes onto the build plate near your cube. Show them that by drawing a square around these multiple shapes you can then move them as a unit.

9. Finally, show them that by highlighting any object and pressing Delete they will remove it from their design. There may be temptation to simply drag an unwanted object off the build plate, but similar to dragging part of your finished design off the build plate in MakerWare, the 3D printer will try to give you what you want by extruding filament for that object you dragged off, ultimately ruining your design.

10. The kids may ask you how long their design will take to print. Reassure them that in this design stage they don't need to worry about how large or small their design is because it can be rescaled to suit the time limit in MakerWare.

11. Let them play around in Tinkercad until their design is complete. Then take a second peek at the design from multiple angles to be sure the various pieces are touching one another and the build plate. If so, then click Download for 3D Printing. Be sure to say the name out loud together. The names in this program are randomly generated total gibberish.

12. Hop into your MakerWare desktop and click Add File, then choose your crazy gibberish name and proceed with your printing!

Dream Big

Time for some free play! For this third and final stage of your 3D demo, it's a good idea to give the kids extra time to print and revisit whichever stage they enjoyed the best. This reinforces the order of operations for printing and really cements their comfort with MakerWare by allowing them to work independently but with you as a resource.

Tab Indicators

STEAM

S: Hypothesizing build times, hypothesizing MakerWare program functions

T: Using equipment: 3D printer, Internet, MakerWare program, Tinkercad program

E: Creating an object using a 3D Printer; learning about moving, turning, viewing, and scaling an object in MakerWare; building a 3D design in Tinkercad

A: Studying objects created using 3D modeling software, designing an object

M: Estimating the size of an object in relation to the amount of time it will take to print, learning about angles on objects and how to support them

Time

20-minute lesson, 60-minute print size

Age level

8+ years

Ingredients

- 3D printer
- 3D printer filament
- Computer hooked up to a 3D printer with Internet access and MakerWare installed

Setup

1. Log into Tinkercad in case that's what the teen wants to use.
2. Have the 3D printer turned on and ready to go.

Instructions

1. Encourage your teens to choose either Thingiverse or Tinkercad to surf around in and create or download a design. Be available to them for questions but let them work independently.
2. Have them tell you when they've either found the object they would like to download or have finished designing their own object.

Double-check that the design or object will work, and encourage them to download and print it. Remind them they have a 60-minute time frame for this challenge and ask if they'd like you to stay. (Even if they say no, be available for questions—just in case!)
3. Help them get the print off when it's complete, and congratulate them on being 3D printer proficient!

Tips and Tricks

- Consider giving out 3D printing licenses to 'tweens and teens who have completed all three steps. With this license they are allowed to ask a librarian to change the color of the filament for their build. It's small, but it means a lot to them. If you have this group's contact information you could also give away extra 3D printing time occasionally!
- Sometimes we offer an Intro to 3D Printing Class where we show off articles that reference the newest cool thing about 3D printing. In the class we cover step 1: Duplicate as a group. Everyone leaves with step 1 complete, even though they didn't actually create the design themselves. It's a great chance for shy kids to complete step 1 and get to know you, and it's a great way for multiple generations of families to get to experience the 3D printer together.
- A thought on sustainability: It may not be feasible for your organization to provide free 3D prints constantly. If you need to charge for this service, don't feel guilty. You could use this intro class as a free primer and then once people have completed it you could add a charge to their card for any future prints. Since the filament is pretty inexpensive it will probably come out to something like 5 or 6 cents per gram.
- You'll probably want to write policies to address any rules you come up with regarding time limits, charging for prints, and perhaps even what objects can be printed. The Internet being what it is you'll find those adorable Pokemon figurines your kids want but you'll also find weapons and pornographic material. It's up to your establishment to determine what is appropriate to print in your children's department. The American Library Association has developed a document called "Progress in the Making," which addresses the different ways 3D printers are being used, concerns like copyright and policy writing for librarians, and further reading: http://www.ala .org/offices/sites/ala.org.offices/files/content/3d_printing_tip sheet_version_9_Final.pdf

Addressing current tech trends is an awesome opportunity libraries have to bridge socioeconomic and technology gaps and provide our young engineers, artists, and visionaries with the tools they need to change the world. It's incredible, big-picture stuff! But we shouldn't simply focus on the highest forms of technology; there are engineering tools all around us, including some of our favorite classic toys. In the next chapter we'll reimagine uses for Legos in new ways to benefit one of the lost groups of the library—'tweens.

6

◇ ◇ ◇

'TWEEN LEGO CLUB

Lego Club is a really fun way to spread a small portion of your programming budget a long way. Kids of all ages love and recognize Legos, they're adaptable for many ages, and the creations from this program can be incorporated into displays, thus building ownership of your library for your 'tween patrons.

'Tweens are a delicate age group and are often forgotten when it comes to programming. Don't let them slip away from you in the time it takes to get from story times to lock-ins. Instead, address the social and educational changes they're going through with programs like the 'Tweens Only Lego Club.

In an educational sense, 'tweens are developmentally ready to experience play with rules. They're still able to enjoy free-building with Legos but enjoy the challenge of games. Emotionally, they're experiencing changes and no longer want to be lumped together with the "little kids"—but they can find teens intimidating. Offering this type of unique programming provides them with a sense of ownership in the library and will cultivate them into teen patrons and active participants.

STOCKING THE PANTRY

- Legos: You'll want a good variety but definitely plan on using 20 to 50 per 'tween per session. These can be donated by patrons, written into a grant, or straight up purchased if you have the budget for it.
- Timer: A kitchen timer or a stopwatch website will work just fine.
- Tables: Enough for workspace for everyone.

- Chairs: One per 'tween
- Space to be silly and laugh in

PROMOTING YOUR PROGRAM

Legos seem to have magical powers. Both kids and parents respond to posters that have Lego images on them, and once you talk up the program and its developmental focuses they're sold. I'd also encourage some 'tweens to volunteer for the library by building some promotional Lego structures for a display to advertise the upcoming launch of the club.

> Creating fun and visible volunteer projects for kids is an incredible way to boost your patronage of kids of all ages, and with all the service projects required for school these days it's a serious win-win!

Another great way to advertise the program is to host it front and center where people can watch how much fun both you and the kids are having. Kids will linger, wondering what's going on, and you can invite them in for a round or two (but be ready for them to stay!).

If your building is in a location where you don't get a lot of foot traffic, consider making a quarter-page flyer that you can send home with kids at school. Plug the club like crazy on your Facebook page and hang posters around town. Remember, Legos have the magic ability to grab the attention of both parents and kids, so use some bold close-up images of Legos in your advertising materials to grab folks' attention right off the bat.

RECIPES

The 60-Second Lego Challenge

This game is the absolute best of the 'Tween Lego Club. 'Tweens are read descriptions of images from books without seeing them. They must guess what you are describing and build it sight unseen. After 60 seconds of building they reveal to the group what they have created and in turn learn what others interpreted the clues to mean. The game highlights your collection and introduces 'tweens to fun facts and subjects they may never have thought about before. Allowing the books you use to be taken home on the spot will help your circulation numbers, too! The time-trial element of building will be a fun new challenge for this age group, and the interpretation of your clues will result in hilarious guesses, incorrect builds, and loads of laughter!

Tab Indicators

STEAM

S: Highlighting science books from your collection, hypothesizing answers based on clues given

T: Highlighting technology books from your collection

E: Highlighting engineering books from your collection, building with Legos

A: Highlighting art books from your collection, creating artistic interpretations of answers to clues given, fostering linguistic processing through abstract play

M: Highlighting math books from your collection, constructing based on size of Legos, counting size of Legos

Time

1 hour

Age level

8 to 12 years

Ingredients

- Tables
- Chairs (one per person)
- Legos
- High-interest nonfiction books

Setup

- Grab some nonfiction books with great images. Mix it up so you've got books about modern art, funky-looking animals, real-life spy gear, and even some abstract ideas (think peace, friendship, and happiness) or invisible bodily functions (think farts, hiccups, and sneezes). Some favorites are listed in the Resources section.
- Set up your chairs around a large table or a cluster of large tables depending on how many kids you anticipate. Groups of 5 or 6 kids per table are ideal and up to 8 to 10 kids per table are manageable.

> The more kids per table the less rounds of the game you'll get to play due to time constraints and the harder it will be to keep everyone focused while still having fun, so plan for what you're comfortable with.

Instructions

1. Each 'tween playing is given one random handful of approximately 20 to 25 Legos to build with. Encourage them to get familiar with

their Lego pieces but not construct anything. Everyone needs to start with all of his or her pieces apart. This is a great time to explain the rules:

a. You will have 60 seconds to build your design.
b. After 60 seconds the leader will yell "Hands up! Designs to the center!" You must do just that. If you continue to build, your design won't be entered in the contest.

Don't be too strict about the time constraint. If they're building for a couple seconds too long it's not the end of the world. On the other hand, if your group is a stickler for the rules, be sensitive to that. In other words, play to your crowd.

c. It is whatever you say it is, even if it's hard for others to see. This means that if you've got a pile of blue Legos that make some random blob and you tell us it's a rhino, then that's what it is. You may be asked to explain the parts of your design so we can "see" it better, but ultimately it is whatever you say it is!
d. When it's time to vote for your favorite, you may vote for any design *except* your own.

Remember, this is fun! If they aren't paying super-close attention because of the Legos, turn their attention back to you in a silly way and then jump back into the rules.

2. This can also be a good time to have the kids introduce themselves if they don't already know one another. Try having them say their name while holding up their favorite piece from their handful.
3. Now it's time for the books. Hide the image you're describing from inside the book. If you want to go bananas you can also hide the covers of the books. Read a description or clues about the image the book gives without giving away the surprise of what you're describing.
4. Once you read the clues (maybe even read them twice) give the kids 60 seconds to build whatever they think you're describing. Let them know when 30 seconds have passed, when 15 seconds remain, and then count down the last 5 seconds. When time is up shout out "Hands up! Designs in the center!" and have them each move their design to the center of the table. (Sometimes it's more like they're pulling the Legos that aren't part of their design away from their build.)
5. Have everyone take a turn describing what he or she built. Some may be dead on and others may be way off. As kids get the hang of the game they may even go totally rogue and build whatever they feel like. If you want you can subtly challenge them to make it relevant to what you were discussing.

6. After everyone has had a turn showing his or her work, you can reveal the image you were referring to and have everyone vote on who built the best replica. Each kid votes for one design that is not his or her own. Now, if you have a bunch of kids and three built giraffes, one built a ninja, and two other kids built rhinos when in fact you were describing a three-toed sloth, this is amazingly funny. Even though no one made a three-toed sloth, ask them to choose "the best three-toed sloth" regardless. It really gets the giggles going. (This is where the 'tweens really stand apart from the "little kids." Most little kids can't see the humor in this situation and some of your younger or more literal 'tweens may also have a hard time at first. Remember to be encouraging, silly, and uplifting.) However, let them "win" from time to time by giving them some easy builds that they'll definitely get right. Whoever gets the most votes each round wins a new handful of Legos. In the event of a tie, give each winner a new handful; if everyone ties, everyone gets a new handful. Prepare yourself for whole group alliances and betrayals!

7. Keep building and switching up the books you use. Always leave them wanting more. Also, feel free to change the time limit as needed, granting an extra 30 seconds here or declaring a challenge so difficult they will get two minutes for their build. Surprises are welcome and will keep the game fresh.

Resources

Web resources:

Lego research: Lego has done fantastic developmental research. It can be really helpful when writing grants or to reference when talking to parents. You should really check it all out, but their 'tween-specific research, "Your 9-11 Year Old Tweens: The Golden Age of Childhood" is found at http://parents.lego.com/en-us /childdevelopment/cd-9-11yrs.

Tweens Only Lego Club blog post for the Chattanooga Public Library: You can check out the piece I wrote up on why we were creating the Lego Club JUST for 'tweens at http://chattlibrary.org/content /tweens-only-lego-club-0.

Free Lego instructions site: Hundreds of build designs are available in one place. Just click and print at http://letsbuilditagain.com /lego-instructions.php!

Great books for this game:

Oooh! Picasso (ISBN 1582462275) and *Oooh! Matisse* (ISBN 1582462275) by Mil Niepold: The experience of playing the 60-Second Lego

Challenge while using these books is a powerful introduction to modern art. The clues are descriptive and vivid, but with a tricky subject like modern art the kids never know what kind of curveball will be thrown at them.

Let's Look At Animal Bottoms by Wendy Perkins (ISBN 0736867155): Any time you can work some potty humor into this program, it's a big hit. Farts, poop, butts, boogers, you name it. If it's something they're not allowed to go into great detail about either at home or in school, let's take advantage and get them giggling! This book is especially great because the kids will either try to make the animal itself or the butt of the animal as a stand-alone object. It leads to tons of laughing and some very creative anatomical creations!

Tell Me a Picture: Adventures in Looking at Art by Quentin Blake (ISBN 1847806422): This one really gets the kids thinking. In it, a small group of people views a work of art and then they ask one another questions about it. Explain to the kids the premise of the book and that the clues are what the people are saying and then read them aloud. After, they'll most likely want to see specifically what parts of the artwork the people were referencing, so it's a win-win. This is a great building tool and a way to get kids talking and thinking critically about art!

Be warned: some 'tweens LOVE this book and others HATE it, but I like to keep it in my arsenal at all times. You never know when the mood will be right, and it'll be the perfect book for that moment!

It's Disgusting and We Ate It! True Food Facts from Around the World and Throughout History by James Solheim (ISBN 0689843933): Another wonderful book for the gross-out factor it possesses, this one will spark some very yucky and creative builds from the kids. In addition, it's a great conversation starter for making new friends and building challenges. "What's the grossest thing YOU ever ate? Build that in the next 60 seconds!"

Anything nonfiction by DK Publishing: DK does a great job of including tons of photos in their nonfiction, and these are described with tidbits of information that make perfect building clues. Since their subjects include pretty much everything they're a great resource to get your Lego Club off the ground and running—and your collection probably already has them! You may even want to theme club gatherings after a while, and these books can be great for that. Some great books to get you started are *Spy Gear, The Roman Empire,* and *Big Cats*!

The One-Hour Build-Off

Once your group has gelled a little, this is a great next step to take with them. They'll have the creativity of free building with the structure of the 60-Second Challenge. The end results can be incredible!

Tab Indicators

STEAM

S: Using books with science themes, experimenting with design elements without all the pieces needed

T: Using books with technology themes

E: Using books with engineering themes, engineering and designing structures based on fiction, reassessing design and building based on pieces available

A: Using books with art themes, creating designs based on literary references, interpreting and referencing book illustrations for design

M: Using books with math themes, counting size of pieces while pulling pieces, counting size of pieces while constructing

Time

1 hour

Age level

8 to 12 years

Ingredients

- Tables
- Chairs (one per person)
- Legos
- High-interest, low-level chapter books

Setup

- Grab some high-interest, low-level chapter books. There are some great ones in the Resources section.
- Set up a story time area. This is a zone where you'll choose the book you want to work from, read a chapter, and then pick a topic. It should be away from where the Legos are.
- Set up two zones: a building zone and a pulling zone.
  - Your pulling zone will be where your 'tweens pull the necessary pieces for whatever they choose to construct.

○ The building zone is where your 'tweens will assemble what-ever pieces they have to create the object or scene they decided to construct.

Instructions

1. Speed-read through a chapter to the group à la story time style. Remind them that the faster you get through the chapter the more time they have to build. Show them any pictures as you read and truly read it out loud and QUICKLY—it's hilarious to them!
2. The kids get three minutes to choose among themselves what scene from the chapter they'd like to recreate using the Legos. You can expect nonsensical arguing, playful banter, and impassioned pleading.
3. There may be a natural division leading 'tweens to want to join either the pulling team or the building team. Go with it if this is the case! If not, divide up your 'tweens somehow while reassuring them that they'll be switching places frequently.
4. Before you leave the story time area, quickly decide upon some pieces everyone can agree on for this build so your pulling team knows how to get started. For example: "We'll need all the black pieces because we're building the night sky and a lot of yellow pieces because we're building the moon."

In the very beginning the building team won't have pieces for a few minutes. While they wait, the building team should discuss their design ideas and communicate the new pieces they'll need to the pulling team.

5. The rest of the hour is spent re-creating your scene from the book with teams simultaneously working. The building team will assemble the design while the pulling team supplies pieces. Every 10 minutes you should have teams switch places so everyone gets time to build. The 'tweens who were in the pulling team will now become the building team, continuing the design that the original building team started, and the 'tweens who were building will now start pulling pieces.
6. When it's all done be sure to get photos of your 'tweens with their creations! It's a great way to improve your social media numbers and to let faraway relatives see what their nieces, nephews, and grandkids are up to!
7. If you want the kids to do their own cleanup, it's best to give it 10 to 15 minutes as there will be an insatiable desire to play with the pieces—even more now that the build-off is over. This time should be tacked on in addition to the hour, otherwise there really isn't enough time to complete the build.

8. Ask the 'tweens if they'd like to do the next chapter of this book the following week when you meet again, maybe even giving them a teaser read of the first few sentences. (Even if they say yes, have a couple of backup books ready in case they change their minds. A lot can happen in a week when you're 11.)

Resources

Here are some great books for this game. I recommend starting with either the first title from each series or the newest title from each series to potentially hook your kids on something new. (And watch your circulation statistics rise for the night!)

Frankie Pickle series by Eric Wright: These are great stories for the one-hour build-off. They're fast paced and have great comic book style pictures and short chapters.

Time Warp Trio series by Jon Scieszka: These are wonderful high-interest, low-level books that are perfect for the One-Hour Build-Off. Especially if your kids are into history or travel, these are great books to consider and have great pictures as references.

Babymouse series by Jennifer Holm and Matthew Holm: Babymouse is a hilarious graphic novel series where all the images are drawn in shades of black, white, and pink. This can be a turnoff for some kids, but I like to present it as a challenge to bring color to her world—much like coloring an old black-and-white movie. If your kids can get past all the pink it can be very fun.

Tips and Tricks

- Assess your group during the 60-Second Lego Challenge. If they're consistently coming up short, feel free to give them a Two-Minute Lego Challenge instead. Unless they're enjoying themselves, they won't get all the benefits of this program—so above all, ensure that they're having a good time!
- If you're ever feeling like your 'tweens are frustrated or the vibe just isn't right, throw in a five-minute "free build" where the 'tweens can make anything they want. It's the magical Lego equivalent of hitting the reset button. In addition, it makes a great opening game if you've got a bunch of new kids one week.
- Pieces go missing. Just like with our book collections there will be pieces that go missing. Some folks may pocket a brick or two in the heat of your white-hot new program and bring it home by accident (and sometimes not so much by accident). Maybe those pieces will

come back and maybe they won't. Really, it's no big deal when you consider you've got hundreds or maybe even thousands of pieces. The fancy pieces (people, flowers, those cool clear bricks you can use to make the best ray guns) can be replaced pretty inexpensively, and you'll be hailed as super cool when you do replace them.

- That's not fair! Because 'tweens are an age group who are only just learning how playing with rules can be fun, they will not always enjoy losing. Occasionally, someone will be having a rough day and feeling like the world is against him or her. Break that tension by acting as Lego fairy and randomly handing out extra bonus pieces. It might be that a 'tween created a design you found to be really clever, and so you reward that, or a really well-constructed design didn't win so you remedy that by throwing a few extra pieces their way. Maybe you give everyone a smattering of fancy pieces because you are a generous fairy. It's a fun way to break the tension and keep everyone happy.

- This club is cool—and fun. And people will want in. That includes the parents of kids who may be too young (or old) for the club. While there certainly are kids who may be educationally developed to the point where they will enjoy the club, they may not be emotionally prepared. The reverse may also be true. I leave it up to you to know how to best lead your program and manage those parents who have the best intentions for their children. However, I will say that if empowering 'tweens is your goal, and you're serious about providing them with something unique and specially built specifically to their needs, be very careful.

If you start allowing younger kids (little brothers or sisters, advanced little ones with pushy parents) to consistently sit in on this club it may (and probably will) be perceived as "boring" or "for babies," and all your hard work will have been lost. Part of what makes this club special for 'tweens is that it's faster paced and has racier subject material than most of your programs for younger kids. Little ones will need you to slow down when reading the clues or won't understand them at all. Your attention will be focused on them because they will need more help to play the games, taking your attention away from those who stand to benefit the most from this club—your 'tweens.

On the flip side, if you start letting teens into the program it can become intimidating for the 'tweens. Teens in a pair or group will overtake the natural conversation that takes place, and most of your 'tweens will stop vocalizing. The simple truth is that teens are bigger, louder, and more developed across the board, and most 'tweens are uncomfortable, stifled, and embarrassed in their presence. If you let teens in you will lose your 'tweens, and your teens will eventually abandon or age out of the club, leaving you with no audience. Don't forget, you're able to use these 'tween-specific programs to farm yourself some invested teen patrons one day. Let your little kids look forward to being old enough to join Lego Club, let your 'tweens have something to look forward to in your teen programs, and encourage your teens to look forward to being adult patrons.

We librarians can have a tendency to be real "yes men," and I am certainly guilty of this. It took me a long time to get to the point where I could commend a parent on being so fabulous and proactive in their child's education as to ask to join an age-inappropriate program and then politely tell them we have other programs available to suit their needs.

This club has a ton of fun, creative energy mixed with physical engineering. In the next chapter we'll mix science and creativity with a dash of fandom as you create your very own *Star Wars* Cooking Club!

7

◇ ◇ ◇

STAR WARS COOKING CLUB

Cooking is an incredible STEAM activity with room for both scientific and artistic experimentation. Mixing *Star Wars* into a cooking program appeals to boys and girls and can get a new audience interested in both your collection of cookbooks and their own culinary potential. While every time you meet you'll be recreating recipes from a few different *Star Wars* cookbooks, there may be times (while things are baking, for example) when you mix in additional activities, such as watching an episode of the cartoon series or coming up with your own clever ideas.

While a lot of the recipes in this chapter involve methods that may be considered taking the easy way out (using premade dough, dressing up already cooked things like hot dogs), remember that it's an introductory class intended to get kids bit by the cooking bug. This could lead to many other cool cooking programs—Mastering Cupcakes, Mason Jar Mix Holiday Gifts, Smoothie Bar Experiments—the possibilities go on and on! Enjoy these early stages and encourage your 'tweens and teens to explore beyond what you do and, more importantly, let you know what they want next for a cooking program.

These days, addressing allergies is a must in any program where food will be offered. It's important for you to know what ingredients are in the foods you'll be preparing and to make that information available to parents should they request it. Since 'tweens or teens will need to sign up in advance for this program, you can ask for a phone number to reach out to parents and ensure that their child will be able to enjoy the program without any health concerns.

STOCKING THE PANTRY

Most of the ingredients you'll want to buy fresh a day or two before your program. As far as cooking equipment goes, you may already have some of these items in your library or classroom. However, in the last example listed here you will need an oven. Feel free to simply borrow kitchen equipment from your home or from coworkers. Don't blow your budget in cooking equipment until you know you'll be offering cooking classes regularly.

Let your budget help dictate your program numbers for this one. Run a cost analysis for each program, and you'll know how many participants you can accept for each class. Keep in mind that number may differ from program to program as the ingredients used change!

PROMOTING YOUR PROGRAM

A fun poster heavy on the *Star Wars* side will draw a crowd for sure. Talking up the program as you're leading 'tweens, teens, and their families to your various *Star Wars* books will both excite them and add a layer of personalization to your customer service. Everyone loves being personally invited to a cool new program. Let your *Star Wars* kids know they're special and you've done something just for them!

Both your posters and your discussions with families should address allergies. If parents have concerns it's always best to be cautious and encourage them to attend other programs you're offering that are better suited to their child's needs.

RECIPES

Yoda Soda

Yoda soda is the perfect first recipe for your new club. It's everything recognizable and wonderful about *Star Wars* mixed with an easy-to-make and tasty treat! Even if you don't have a kitchen you can create this delicious concoction anywhere. Also, if you don't want to do an entire series on *Star Wars* cooking it's a great stand-alone program.

As a first-level lesson your kids will experiment with measuring and mixing, two of the most fun parts of cooking and a great way to get them bit by the cooking bug!

I've found that the recipe in the book is a good jumping-off point but can also be tweaked to fit your needs. If limes are super expensive the week of the program, feel free to scale back. The kids will still get to experience juicing, and after all, this class is an introduction to cooking techniques, not a master's class! The flavors from the sorbet and sugar will be plenty to keep them happy.

Tab Indicators

STEAM

S: Mixing ingredients, experimenting with flavors
T: Using cooking equipment
E: Physically creating a recipe, extracting ingredients through juicing
A: Adjusting recipe for flavor/color
M: Measuring ingredients, adding or multiplying to have a variety of measuring cups equal one cup

Time

1 hour

Age level

8+ years

Ingredients

- A surface for your participants to work on
- Sparkling water (1 cup per participant)
- Sugar (3 Tbsp per person)
- Limes (a half to one lime per participant)
- Lime sherbet (or any other flavor if you can't get your hands on lime) (one scoop per person)
- Hand-held juicer

The juicer is not necessary but definitely fun to play with! If you can borrow one for this the kids will love playing with it. If not, they'll be able to squeeze the lime juice manually.

- Sharp knife
- Clear cups
- Cutting board
- Spoons (just regular old spoons for stirring and mixing)
- Measuring spoons
- Measuring cups
- A sink or series of wash buckets to rinse measuring cups and spoons in so they can be reused by participants
- Dish towels or paper towels
- Straws

- Trash cans
- Book: *The Star Wars Cookbook: Wookiee Cookies and Other Galactic Recipes* by Robin Davis (ISBN 0811821846)
- A sign-up sheet to participate in the next *Star Wars* Cooking Club event
- Instructions for each station (See suggestions at the end of the Resources section for instruction card ideas)

Setup

Set up your work space procession-line style into the following stations with the necessary equipment:

1. Station 1: Equipment
   a. Clear plastic cups
   b. Measuring spoons
   c. Measuring cups
   d. Mixing spoon
   e. Instructions
2. Station 2: Mixing
   a. Limes

> You may want to cut your limes in half before this program begins. Otherwise you can have a volunteer you trust do this or designate it a parent task, whatever works for you!

   b. Hand-held juicer
   c. Cutting board
   d. Sugar
   e. Paper towels
   f. Instructions
3. Station 3: Stirring Bubbles
   a. Sherbet
   b. Ginger ale
   c. Straws
   d. Instructions
4. Station 4: Cleanup
   a. A sink or series of wash buckets (one with warm soapy water and two more with warm water for rinsing)
   b. Towels or paper towels for drying dishes
   c. Instructions
5. Station 5: Enjoyment!
   a. Tables and/or chairs where folks can sit and enjoy their treats

Have trash cans ready near your exits for participants to throw away their rubbish as they leave.

Instructions

1. Welcome your participants and tell them that besides offering a lesson in how to create today's recipe, you'll also be giving a beginner's lesson on using cooking equipment and best practices for cooking. Encourage your parent participants to share their own family's cooking tips with their children—but not to interrupt the main lesson, please.
2. All participants should now wash their hands. I like to refer to the CDC's guide (available in the Resources section) for hand washing and have everyone sing "Happy Birthday" during the scrubbing of their hands.
3. Start by having everyone watch you as you walk through the stations and explain what they'll do at each one. Be sure to highlight the cooking lessons they'll be participating in today as the basics of learning to cook:
   a. Measuring
   b. Juicing
   c. Stirring
   d. Mixing
4. You'll also want to point out if your measuring cups are multiple sizes. They will need to do the math to come up with a one-cup measurement at Station 3.

If possible, please DO provide measuring cups in every size BUT one cup! This adds another layer of math to this program.

5. When pointing out Station 5, where folks can sit and enjoy their soda at the end, encourage them to discuss cooking notes with one another and talk about what they would do differently with this recipe in the future.
6. Ask participants to begin!
7. While the program is taking place, be available to answer questions, help out 'tweens and teens, and just have fun! Keep sparking the conversation by asking how participants would change the recipe if it were up to them or what they might use their newfound recipe skills for in the future!
8. Finally, before folks start to leave, advertise that during your next cooking program you'll be making Jawa Jive Milk Shakes and playing with more advanced cooking equipment. They won't be able to resist! Have your sign-up sheet for next time ready to go because people will want to lock down their spots ASAP.

Resources

"When & How to Wash Your Hands," CDC's guide to hand washing: http://www.cdc.gov/handwashing/when-how-handwashing.html

BONUS! There are some truly excellent posters to encourage hand washing at CDC's site, including a batch with literary references from famous authors! Score! (See http://www.cdc.gov/handwashing/posters.html.)

Station 1 Instructions

Welcome, Earthlings!
Take the following items with you on your journey, you must:

- One tablespoon
- One measuring cup
- One cup
- One spoon
- One straw

Station 2 Instructions

- Step 1: Measure 3 Tbsp of sugar into your cup
- Step 2: Juice half a lime into your cup (or whatever amount you land on!)
- Step 3: Mix sugar and juice together with your spoon or straw

Station 3 Instructions

- Step 1: Place a scoop of sherbet into your cup
- Step 2: Measure one cup of bubbly water (Be careful to do the math for whatever size measuring cup you have!)
- Step 3: Pour bubbly water into your cup
- Step 4: Stir ingredients together
- Step 5: Rinse and dry your measuring cup and measuring spoon at the next station and bring them back to Station 1

Station 4 Instructions

- Step 1: Rinse your measuring cup and measuring spoon
- Step 2: Dry your measuring cup and measuring spoon
- Step 3: Return your measuring cup and measuring spoon to Station 1
- Step 4: Enjoy your Yoda Soda!

Jawa Jive Milk Shakes

In this lesson we stray a bit from what's printed on the cookbook pages but highlight the recipe. This does two things. First, it encourages 'tweens and teens to check the book out and recreate some more recipes at home. Second, it shows them that you don't always have to create exactly what's on the page when it comes to cooking.

This time, you're upping the ante by adding a blender into the mix. (Thank you, thank you. Pun completely intended.) The blender is sent from heaven when it comes to this age group—it's loud, covered in buttons, and provides instant gratification. It's like the gods smiled down on you and granted you with cooking superpowers.

Tab Indicators

STEAM
S: Mixing ingredients, experimenting with flavors, experimenting with blender speeds, experimenting with techniques to disassemble candy
T: Using cooking equipment
E: Physically creating a recipe, adjusting the setting on the blender to perform with chosen ingredients, disassembling candy to prepare for blending
A: Adjusting recipe for flavor/color
M: Measuring ingredients, assessing how small to make the candy

Time
1 hour

Age level
8+ years

Ingredients
- A surface for your participants to work on
- Blender
- Clear cups (one per person)
- Bowls (one per type of candy)
- Spoons (one per person, one per bowl of candy, one to scoop ice cream)
- Straws (one per person)
- Milk (¼ cup per person)
- Ice cream (one cup per person)
- Random candy to be "space garbage" (items that work well: marshmallows, sprinkles, Kit Kats, chocolate chips, M&Ms)

Keeping these nut free is a good idea to avoid allergy problems, but read your packages. If you are using anything that says it may contain traces due to being processed in a plant where nuts are used, this needs to be communicated to parents of allergic children!

- Instructions for each station (see suggestions at the end of the Resources section for instruction card ideas)

Of course there are healthy alternatives for this, too—you can use bananas, peanut butter, honey, spinach, fresh or frozen berries, raisins, or whatever you like!

- Sealable plastic bags
- Rolling pin
- Cutting board
- A kitchen knife or kitchen scissors
- Plastic knives (one per person)
- Measuring spoons
- Measuring cups (make sure you have a variety but definitely include a few ¼ cup)
- A sink or series of wash buckets to rinse measuring cups and spoons in so they can be reused by participants
- Dish towels or paper towels
- Trash cans
- Book: *The Star Wars Cookbook: Wookiee Cookies and Other Galactic Recipes* by Robin Davis (ISBN 0811821846)
- A sign-up sheet to participate in the next *Star Wars* Cooking Club event

Setup

Set up your work space production-line style into the following stations with the necessary equipment:

1. Station 1: Equipment
   a. Clear plastic cups
   b. Measuring spoons
   c. Measuring cups
   d. Mixing spoon
   e. Instructions
2. Station 2: Prep Work
   a. Plastic knives
   b. Cutting board
   c. "Space garbage" candy
      i. Candy divided into bowls
      ii. Spoon in each bowl
   d. Sealable plastic bags
   e. Rolling pin
   f. Instructions

3. Station 3: Mixing
   a. Ice cream (you can keep it cold by placing it in a bucket of ice)
   b. Milk (you can keep it cold by placing it in a bucket of ice)
   c. Blender
   d. Instructions
4. Station 4: Cleanup
   a. A sink or series of wash buckets (one with warm soapy water and two more with warm water for rinsing)
   b. Towels or paper towels for drying dishes
   c. Instructions
5. Station 5: Enjoyment!
   a. Tables and/or chairs where folks can sit and enjoy their treats

Have trash cans ready near your exits for participants to throw away their rubbish as they leave.

Instructions

1. Welcome your participants and tell them that today's lesson will involve more cooking equipment. They'll need to use their measuring and mixing skills from last time and will experiment today with a rolling pin and blender.
2. Time to wash hands! It's a great time to discuss how starting with clean hands is starting with a germ-free canvas and to mention the FDA's hand-washing guidelines. I like to refer to the CDC's guide for hand washing and have everyone sing "Happy Birthday" during the scrubbing of their hands.
3. Just like last time you'll want to do a quick demonstration explaining the sequence of the stations and what to do at each station.
4. Have participants get started! Again, make yourself available to offer help, answer questions, and just be available for whatever may come.

The Mixing Station may become bottlenecked. Encourage folks not to nibble too much on their candy as they wait and keep an eye on whether or not the blender needs an extra splash of milk to really get things moving.

5. Before folks start to leave, advertise that your next cooking program will be creating Darth Maul's Double Dogs! This does mean meat, which your patrons who are vegetarians may need to know; however, you could always offer a tofu version if your population is heavily vegetarian! Have your sign-up sheet for next time ready to go.

Resources

Station 1 Instructions

Welcome, Earthlings!

Take the following items with you on your journey, you must:

- One measuring cup
- One cup
- One spoon
- One straw

Station 2 Instructions

- Step 1: Choose candy ("space garbage") for your milk shake. You may have one scoop of each kind.

The amount of candy each milk shake gets is up to you and depends on how much candy you have.

- Step 2: Using knives or kitchen scissors, cut apart full-sized candy bars and large-sized marshmallows to a size you're happy to add to your milk shake.
- Step 3: If you choose a crumbly, cookie-type candy you'll want to crush it. Put it inside a plastic bag and SEAL IT with almost no air inside. Use the rolling pin to crush the candy by rolling over the sealed bag.

Station 3 Instructions

- Step 1: Measure ½ cup of milk and pour it into the blender.
- Step 2: Measure one cup ice cream and put it in the blender.
- Step 3: Pour your candy on top of the ice cream and milk.
- Step 4: Fit the lid of the blender on TIGHTLY.
- Step 5: Read the settings on the front of the blender to mix up your milk shake!

Station 4 Instructions

- Step 1: Rinse your measuring cup
- Step 2: Dry your measuring cup
- Step 3: Return your measuring cup to Station 1 and enjoy your milk shake!

Darth Double Dogs

This final recipe has a lot of wow factor and is sure to produce some super-silly fun and photos! For those who don't know, Darth Maul famously had a double-sided red light saber. Two foot-long hot dogs capped in the middle with some elaborate pastry will teach your 'tweens and teens a bit about how pastry rises and spreads out when cooking while recreating this amazing relic of *Star Wars* history. The skewer is not part of the original recipe from the book but will provide the support needed to actually lift the double light saber, not just flop it off a plate without the opportunity to play with your food. This recipe will either finish your multiweek program with a bang or spark interest in continuing. The choice is yours!

Unlike the other two recipes we've looked at, this one does require an oven. The oven is the most advanced piece of cooking equipment they'll learn about in this class, but it also means you'll actually need a kitchen to pull this program off.

Tab Indicators

STEAM

S: Hypothesizing the spread of pastry when designing and constructing handles, hypothesizing how long dogs and handles will take to cook based on the amount of pastry used.

T: Using cooking equipment

E: Physically creating a recipe, constructing core to hold dogs together, measuring the balance of the core between dogs

A: Styling dough for the handle, creatively re-creating fight scenes with the finished recipe!

M: Measuring pastry components, counting ingredients, learning about temperature gauges on an oven, learning about timers on an oven

Time

1 hour

Age level

8+ years

Ingredients

- A surface for your participants to work on
- Foot-long hot dogs (red-colored hot dogs are best but aren't available in every state; don't sweat it if you can't get your hands on red ones) (one per person or two if you want to go more realistic)
- Paper plates to work on (one per person)
- Skewers (one per person)
- Packaged crescent rolls (two rolls per person)
- Dish towels or paper towels
- Trash cans
- Book: *The Star Wars Cookbook II: Darth Malt and More Galactic Recipes* by Frankie Frankeny (ISBN 0811828034)
- A sign-up sheet to receive information on your next cooking program
- An oven
- Scrap paper or parchment paper
- Pencils
- Two or three baking sheets
- Butter knives, plastic works just fine (one per person)
- Mustard
- Ketchup
- Projector setup, television viewing area, or whatever you have to access an episode of *Star Wars: The Clone Wars*
- Seats or comfy floor space to watch an episode of *Star Wars: The Clone Wars* (Episodes run for about 22 minutes, so there's a perfect amount of time to start your baking and then go check on your progress during the spots where commercial breaks would be.)
- Any episode of *Star Wars: The Clone Wars* cartoon to watch (So long as it's covered under your library or school's movie license!)

Setup

1. Unlike other *Star Wars* Cooking Classes, you'll probably need to limit your number of participants for this program. Take a good look at your oven and be honest with yourself about how many two-foot light sabers you'll be able to fit in AT ONE TIME. It's tempting to want to do two rounds, but they'll cook at different times based on how much dough is used (and dough usage WILL vary). Trust me. Just get through one round of dogs. Don't keep people waiting. Don't promise what you can't deliver, and everyone will be much happier. Don't forget—you can always do this again!
2. Arrange your work space with tables and chairs so everyone can see one another and what they're working on.
3. Each participant's spot should have a paper plate, a skewer, and a knife.
4. Have trash cans ready near your exits for participants to throw away their rubbish as they leave.
5. If you're offering ketchup and mustard, they can just be set up randomly around the tables.
6. Get your viewing area ready and be prepared for people to want to eat in it.

Instructions

1. Welcome your participants and let them know that today they'll be cooking in the oven—a standard piece of cooking equipment in every kitchen. Ovens are a great piece of equipment to know how to use, and today you'll go over some of the basics of how they work. But kids should NEVER use an oven without a parent's permission AND supervision. Your participants should always ASK to use an oven.
2. Time to wash hands! It's a great time to discuss how starting with clean hands is starting with a germ-free canvas and to mention the FDA's hand-washing guidelines. I like to refer to the CDC's guide for hand washing and have everyone sing "Happy Birthday" during the scrubbing of their hands. You've done this a couple times now and don't want folks to be bored. If you see that's happening, see if they can keep the tune but switch up the lyrics for fun.
3. Start by preheating the oven to 375 degrees. Don't just run over and turn it on though, walk participants through how ovens typically have a light that goes on or off once the oven is preheated and to show what will happen with your oven. You can also point out that some ovens run off gas and others electricity, then explain what kind of oven you'll be using today and how they can tell the difference.

4. Pull your ingredients out of the fridge and get some helpers to carry them to your work area for you.
5. Have whoever carried the hot dogs deliver two hot dogs to each person.
6. Have your crescent-roll helper deliver the necessary amount of cans per table based on how many rolls are inside each can.
7. In a place where everyone can see, demonstrate that the basic construction of Darth Maul's Double Dogs is two foot-long hot dogs touching long ways. They are skewered together in the middle and then wrapped with one crescent roll to cover the seam of the dogs touching and create a handle.
8. Participants will have the basics to create this recipe but will also have an additional crescent roll to use for decorating their handles.

While not necessary, embellishing the handles with extra dough will help distinguish between all the double dogs you'll be baking. Otherwise, I recommend drawing yourself a little map on scrap paper to keep track of whose dog is where or, better yet, baking them on parchment paper and having the kids write their names next to their dogs when they place it!

9. Explain that when pastry dough cooks it spreads, so very fine or intricate designs will get puffy and distorted. Simple shapes work best, but they should feel free to experiment and see what happens! An average crescent roll takes 10 to 12 minutes to cook. Have them keep this in mind when getting creative—a very thick layer of dough will take much longer to cook and may even result in a burnt hot dog.
10. As a final instruction let them know that when they're totally done assembling their double dogs they should bring them up to you for placement on the baking tray.
11. Now let participants dig into their ingredients and get assembling! Make yourself available to help open the crescent roll containers (They pop—what fun! Your young chefs will love this!), give advice, and joke around.
12. As participants finish their double dogs and bring them up to you it will be helpful to have a piece of scrap paper available for you to use to draw a map of where each person's dog is located on the tray or to use parchment paper they can write their names on next to their dogs. It's also fun to have them make a hypothesis about how long they believe their dog will take to cook.
13. When you've collected enough double dogs for your first baking tray, have everyone head to the oven (which is hopefully preheated by now!). Demonstrate how to safely open the oven and place the dogs inside, and then show how to set the timer and how you'll

know when the dogs are done. It's also helpful to give tips like watching for their handles to turn golden brown. Typically, a hot dog wrapped in a crescent roll will take 10 to 12 minutes to bake according to Pillsbury's website, but you'll have some extra dough on your handles so they may require a little more time. Make a note on your map with the group about what time you put the dogs in. This will come in handy later when those with the really thick handles keep baking and baking and baking and you need to tell your little Jedi how long their dog took to cook in total.

> You can expect the dogs to finish at different times. Their positions in the oven mixed with the amount of dough used causes them to cook at different rates. As the dogs finish, reposition the remaining dogs to cook more in the center of the oven and explain to your 'tweens and teens what you're doing.

14. Have participants whose dogs are in the oven go to the viewing area and get ready to see their finished masterpieces. Get another tray into the oven, run the second group through the same routine, and send them to the viewing area too. Start an episode and have participants follow you to the oven to see the dogs' progress where commercial breaks would be.

> Having two groups of dogs that start at two different times means some math for you. Keep track of it and continue to point out to participants how they can tell when dogs are done by their color.

15. As dogs begin to finish, encourage folks to let them cool down before grabbing and eating them. (OK, let's be realistic. They're totally gonna play with their food as long as possible before eating it!) Have your ketchup and mustard ready to go and plenty of paper towels at the ready. Grab some great photos and enjoy!
16. Finally, before folks start to leave, ask them to leave feedback on what kind of cooking program you should offer next. More *Star Wars* recipes? Move on to real baking? Have them write their suggestions and contact information on your sheet.

Tips and Tricks

- If that last recipe sounded like too much to you, simplify it and give each participant one hot dog and one crescent roll. Have them wrap the middle of their hot dog with the roll and leave out the embellishment part. Bake them the same way and enjoy!

- Don't forget to check your movie license to be sure you're covered to watch episodes of *The Clone Wars* legally. For more information on this, check out the chapter titled Movie Release Events.
- For the Jawa Jive Milk Shakes, it's fun to label your space garbage if you have the time. Chocolate chips can be Rancor Poop, marshmallows can be Tauntaun Boogers, Kit Kats can be Trash Compactor Debris, sprinkles can be Ewok Dandruff, M&M's can be Wookiee Kibble (those are Ws! Not Ms!), or they can be separated by color and labeled with your own fun ideas!

The artistic and scientific basis of cooking can lead to so many other creative programs. Crowd-sourcing with your attendees will lead you in such cool directions. One possibility is what I've outlined in the next chapter, a deeper exploration of science in the real world tackling the hot topics of crime scene investigation and forensic science using real tools of the trade!

8

CSI SCIENCE

The forensic science bug bit our nation in 2000, and CSI fever has spread like wildfire ever since. On top of bringing some intriguing science experiments to the table, this program is also a fun way to build a relationship between your police department and your patrons and your library. For your 'tweens and teens, having a real police officer discuss with them how forensic or investigative practices are used will be thrilling. For your police officers, it's an incredible opportunity to highlight the cool work they do in a positive setting. Your library will experience the benefit of connecting with teens and your local police force, enhancing all three relationships. You feeling those good vibes yet?

STOCKING THE PANTRY

While the items listed here aren't super expensive, they can add up quickly depending on how many times you want your teens and 'tweens to get to experience them. Willing to have the group watch as one person demonstrates? You'll get by with one of each. Want everyone who comes to do all the activities? Get ready to start spending! However, you mix all the STEAM goodness of this program with the pop culture buzz surrounding forensics *and* the mentorship of local police and you've got a super-strong grant application on your hands!

Police Officers

If you or any of your coworkers already have a good relationship with some local officers, just call them up and ask! If there are no existing relationships with officers, call the station and explain who you are, that you're calling because you're interested in setting up an after-school program to explain some basic forensic experiments to 'tweens and teens and that you'd like an officer's presence to lend an air of validity to the program and to build relationships between kids and officers based in learning and fun. Ask whom you should contact about this and when would be a good time to contact this person. Don't forget, these officers are busy! You'll want to call at least a month in advance so you both have time to schedule something that works for you and so that you have enough time to properly market this program. When the time comes and you're talking to the correct person, let your officer know the following:

- Give a brief rundown of the program you will be presenting.
- The police officer will be talking for approximately 20 minutes on a forensic topic of his or her choice.
- You would like to know what topic they would like to discuss before the day of the program. This will allow you to find materials to support the officer's talk, be it books, articles to share, or maybe even a new activity of your own design!
- You would like to know if the officer would be interested in bringing any equipment to show off.
- You would like time for questions at the end of the officer's talk.
- You would like the officer to stay and participate with the 'tweens and teens in the forensic experiments following the talk.

pH Analysis

pH levels can be tested to discover the presence of a decaying body in soil or drugs in blood or to identify illegally polluted water. pH stands for "potential hydrogen." Not only are the results of such tests helpful in solving obvious crimes but they can also be used in other ways. For example, the pH levels of mud found on a suspect's shoes can be measured and compared with the pH results of mud from a crime scene. Unfortunately, unlike fingerprint evidence, pH levels change quickly. As such, it's important to get samples tested in a timely manner. A great eBook for your kids is *Forensic Science, Grades 6-8* by Jeanette Jolley and John Powrie.

pH Strips

Packages typically contain between 80 and 100 strips and can be purchased at any pool store or online. An Amazon search revealed dozens of options at multiple price points.

Fingerprint Analysis

Fingerprint evidence is used to identify criminals who have left evidence of their fingerprints behind at the scene of a crime. No two people have the same fingerprints, and the patterns of our prints remain the same throughout our entire lives. With advancements in technology, fingerprints can now be scanned digitally and submitted into a national database called the Integrated Automated Fingerprint Identification System, or IAFIS for short.

Fingerprint Powder

This can be found online. You'll want to purchase one container for every two participants. Latent print powder packs can be purchased from CrimeScene.com: http://www.crimescene.com/store/index.php?main_page=product_info&products_id=350.

Fingerprint Dusting Brush

These can be found online, such as this one at CrimeScene.com: http://www.crimescene.com/store/index.php?main_page=product_info&products_id=57.

Fingerprint Lifting Tape

Fingerprint lifting pads like you see on TV are just precut fingerprint lifting tape. You can purchase single 2" × 2" pads, an entire roll of the tape costs about the same (http://www.crimescene.com/store/index.php?main_page=product_info&products_id=77)! If your budget is tight try using clear packing tape.

Footwear Analysis

Footwear impressions left behind at the scene of the crime can help identify criminals who left those prints and exclude suspects who were not present. Class characteristics and identifying characteristics are both used when identifying footwear that actually left the impressions at the scene of the crime. Class characteristics are manufacturing details of footwear—the size, design, and molded shapes. Identifying characteristics are accidental and unintentional markings of the footwear, such as rocks, thumbtacks or tape stuck in the shoe or cuts, and gouges or scuffs to the shoe. For more from the FBI on footwear analysis, see "The Forensic Analysis of Footwear Impression Evidence" by Michael B. Smith at http://www.fbi.gov/about-us/lab/forensic-science-communications/fsc/july2009/review/2009_07_review02.htm.

Footwear Impression Kit

These can be purchased online, such as this one: http://www.crimescene .com/store/index.php?main_page=product_info&cPath=60&products _id=128.

PROMOTING YOUR PROGRAM

Your poster and word of mouth will do a great job getting 'tweens and teens interested in this program. Your poster should be dark and gritty; images of crime tape or a CSI team are great visuals!

If you want to go further you can create a masking tape outline and put up some caution tape to make a crime scene. Put up a bunch of your books on famous crimes, detectives, detective work, and forensics to really drive the point home. Plus, it makes for fascinating discussions at the program when students find out officers don't use chalk outlines for bodies!

RECIPES

CSI Science

Your teens and 'tweens will love the opportunity to handle and experiment with the real equipment that police officers and forensic scientists use to do their jobs. Setup is quick, the price is flexible, and real police involvement adds an air of reality. When it's over they'll want to know immediately when it's happening again!

Tab Indicators

STEAM

- S: Learning basic chemistry principles of pH levels, hypothesizing outcomes of experiments, analyzing test results to arrive at conclusions
- T: Using police equipment
- E: Dusting for fingerprints, lifting fingerprints, creating footwear impressions
- A: Drawing fingerprints
- M: Analyzing pH number results, identifying patterns in footwear impressions

Time

1 hour

Age level

8 to 18 years

Ingredients

- Tables with enough space to set up three different experiments
- An area for your teens and 'tweens to watch the police officer's talk without being distracted by the experiments
- 8.5" × 11" printouts of common patterns in fingerprints (arches, loops, and whorls) taped to the wall near the fingerprint station
- Pencils
- Paper
- Tape
- Spray cleaner and paper towels (to clean up afterward)
- Police officer(s)
- Bottled water for the officer(s)

Tips for getting a good reputation when it comes to handling speakers:

1. Always send the speaker a notice about where to park to unload equipment and where to park after unloading.
2. Always offer to help unload the equipment! Or try to line up staff or volunteers who can assist.
3. Always offer a refreshment when the speaker arrives and if he or she drinks it while talking, teaching, or performing, don't ask, just bring another!
4. Always send a thank-you note, and if you enjoyed the talk, lesson, or performance offer to be a reference in the future!

pH Station

- One table
- pH strips (one per person)
- Can of diet cola
- Can of regular cola
- Two plastic cups: one labeled "Diet" with diet cola in it and the other labeled "Cola" with the regular cola in it
- A copy of each Results Card per person, so three cards total per person. (These are available in the Resources section.)

Shoe Print Station

- Footwear Impression Kit
- Sneakers (the more similar the treads the better!)
- Results Card (one per participant)

Fingerprint Station

- Two tables
- Small cups (like the paper ones in bathrooms or the free kind you can grab for ketchup at a fast food place)
- Paper to practice taking fingerprints (scrap is fine!)
- Pencils
- Fingerprint dusting powder divided into small cups
- Fingerprint lifting tape
- Fingerprint dusting brushes (one per participant would be the best, but one for every two participants will work)
- Index cards or paper to tape fingerprints onto (one per participant)
- Results Card (one per participant)

Setup

1. It's a good idea to practice lifting fingerprints so you can demonstrate how it's done later. In fact, why not have a little fun and play with the pH strips, too!
2. Set up the stations listed earlier with the equipment listed. These stations should be away from where the officer is talking so they're visible when the participants enter the room but not distracting while the officer is talking.
3. Now that you know the topic the officer will be discussing, do a little research on it to come up with a few questions for him or her.
   a. If you're feeling unsure about asking questions relating to the topic, these are always helpful:
      i. What's involved in becoming a police officer?
      ii. Is it very different to become a forensic scientist?
      iii. What would you say is the main difference between the investigative work you do as an officer and that of forensic scientists?
      iv. If you could debunk one myth that's perpetuated through the various crime shows on television what would it be?

Instructions

1. Introduce your officer! Welcome the officer and let your participants know the forensic subject he or she will be speaking about today.
2. Let the officer do his or her thing!
3. Invite the 'tweens and teens to ask questions when the officer has finished. If they don't have any, you can ask some from your research to get the ball rolling.

4. When questions are done, explain that everyone will get to try his or her hand at pH testing and lifting fingerprints today, and the group will all watch the footprint impression performed by two participants—those with the best behavior, those chosen by random drawing, or whatever method you choose.

5. Review the concept of hypothesis. Explain that it is an educated guess based on what we already know. Let them know they'll each be making three hypotheses today, one for each experiment.

6. On your own head over to the Fingerprint Experiment. Explain that everyone knows that no two fingerprints are alike but there are similar patterns within fingerprints. These patterns are arches, loops, and whorls.

If your officer chose to speak about fingerprints, you don't need to repeat everything he or she just said. Instead, explain how they'll use the dusting powder and tape and point out that you have examples of the typical fingerprint patterns available on the wall for them to identify in the prints they lift.

7. Using paper, have all participants take their own fingerprints, write their names on their sheets, and tape them up on the wall.

8. Explain that they'll each get a chance to lift fingerprints from the room. Show the cups of powder and brushes and demonstrate once how to brush, lift, and tape down a fingerprint onto the Results Card. Explain that using the card they'll hypothesize whose fingerprint they have and then try to match them up! The center area of their Results Card is where they'll write down whose print they actually have, if they can figure it out! The final question about how this could be used should be fairly evident but because of this their answers might actually wind up being pretty funny.

Chances are they won't find a fingerprint match, but that in itself is a good lesson—there's a lot more work to finding a match than many crime TV shows would lead you to believe.

9. Now head over to the pH station. Explain that a pH strip works by measuring the amount of pH (potential hydrogen) in a substance. The less hydrogen the more acidic the solution. pH is measured on a scale of 0 to 14, in which 0 to 7 is the acidic side of the scale and 8 to 14 is the alkaline side of the scale. Both extreme sides of the scale can be harmful to humans. For example, lye, which is used to make soap, can cause severe burns and is on the very alkaline side of the scale at 13. Battery acid comes in at the other end at a 2.2. Distilled

water has a pH of 7. Human blood has a pH of about 7.3. Teens and 'tweens will be using strips that measure pH by inserting them into the cups of liquid.

10. Pass out the pH Experiment Results Cards. Explain that on this card they will need to write down their hypothesis for which liquid they believe will be more acidic, cola or diet cola, and why. Then they'll run the experiment by following the instructions on the pH strips container. They'll record their results and then write down an example of where this kind of experiment would be useful in police work.

11. Set the 'tweens and teens free to try their hands at both experiments!

12. Before starting the experiment have your teens and 'tweens fill out their Footwear Impression Results Card. This time they'll be hypothesizing on how clear the footprint will be and determining if their guess was correct after the impression has been made and is passed around.

13. Choose your two best behaved or randomly drawn students to come up to the front of the class to demonstrate the footwear impression kit. One will hold the impression kit and the other will step into it.

This is another great area to have the officer help with. Especially if the officer is familiar with this kind of kit, he or she can teach the students how to use the kit. If the officer is not familiar, simply ask if he or she would be willing. This part is going to get some laughs if for nothing more than one wobbly, flamingo-legged student trying to make the impression. It's great to end the program with a laugh, and to have your officer be a part of generating it will be great for his or her reputation afterward.

14. When the impression is made, pass it around the group so they can jot down their results, and either write or discuss as a group useful ways this test could be used in crime scene investigation.

15. When you've got about 10 minutes left in your hour together, have the teens and 'tweens reconvene where the officer spoke. Ask if anyone wants to share a hypothesis and results. Allow them to share and get a little loud, laughing about who had the same answers, who got it wrong, their wacky ideas on how these tests could be used, etc.

16. Thank your officer for joining you, lead a big round of applause for the officer, and invite everyone to take their Results Cards home and check out books from the awesome display you made if they want more information on CSI or forensics work!

17. After everyone's gone take a look at the remaining Results Cards and check out some of their answers, you may find some gems! These also make great social media fodder!

Resources

FBI Overview on Fingerprints & Biometrics: http://www.fbi.gov
/about-us/cjis/fingerprints_biometrics

Forensic Science, Grades 6-8 by Jeanette Jolley and John Powrie: http://
books.google.com/books/about/Forensic_Science_Grades_6_8
.html?id=qmYb_16W8P8C

A Simplified Guide to Forensic Science, assembled by the National
Forensic Science Testing Center and Bureau of Justice Assistance, is available on the website (http://www.forensicsciencesimplified.org/statement
.html) and as an eBook (http://www.nfstc.org/bja-programs/forensic
-science-simplified/).

Fingerprint Experiment
Results Card

Hypothesis:

Results:

Ways I could see this test being used:

pH Experiment
Results Card

Hypothesis:

Results:

Ways I could see this test being used:

Footwear Experiment
Results Card

Hypothesis:

Results:

Ways I could see this test being used:

From *Cooking Up Library Programs Teens and 'Tweens Will Love: Recipes for Success* by Megan Emery Schadlich. Santa Barbara, CA: Libraries Unlimited. Copyright © 2015.

Tips and Tricks

- While this program can easily be run in just one hour, you can also split it into two separate programs and offer even more information to your kids. You'll want to participate in the forensic experiment that matches your officer's talk on the first day, and on the second day you can do the two remaining experiments.

- If you have no officer to come and talk to your kids you can still run this program. I'd suggest leaving a good 15 minutes to talk about fingerprints, 10 minutes to talk about pH, and 10 minutes to talk about the footwear impressions. If you're not super comfortable with discussing this without an expert you can add a few items and host a CSI Petting Zoo for the first part of your program. The Idea behind a Petting Zoo is not that your 'tweens and teens would get to run individual experiments like the ones designed in this chapter. Instead, it's an opportunity for them to handle the equipment used by many police officers and CSI daily. This kind of hands-on experience will allow them to see the amount of information that is required to be written down to submit evidence, to touch theft detection powder and see the stain it makes on their hands, and to actually open a swab detection collector, to write with a UV pen and then see its mark using a UV flashlight. Basically, it's a chance to touch some of the gear they've seen used on TV. Here are some more inexpensive items you can add that teens and 'tweens will love getting to handle:

  - DNA collection swabs with caps: Can be purchased online at http://www.crimescene.com/store/index.php?main_page=product_info&cPath=23&products_id=386
  - Evidence envelope: Can be purchased online at http://www.crimescene.com/store/index.php?main_page=product_info&cPath=52&products_id=804
  - Theft detection powder: Can be purchased online at http://www.crimescene.com/store/index.php?main_page=product_info&cPath=54&products_id=48
  - UV marking pens: Can be purchased online at http://www.crimescene.com/store/index.php?main_page=product_info&cPath=54&products_id=358
  - UV flashlight: Can be found on Amazon.com, for example, http://www.amazon.com/Professional-Inspection-Flashlight-380-385nm-Ultraviolet/dp/B0013E3XVU
  - Kits: The crimescene.com webside also sells a variety of kits ranging in price and activity (Drug busts! Blood analysis! Solving a murder!). If your kids love your CSI program, it may be worth the

cost of such a kit to run a more in-depth experience for them in the future. CrimeScene.com kits may be found here: http://www.crimescene.com/store/index.php?main_page=index&cPath=50&sort=20a&page=2 .

Like most of my programs, you'll benefit a LOT from talking to your teens about what they're enjoying and what they'd like to repeat from this program. Do they want to see a mobile forensics lab? Would they like to play with luminol? Are they interested in having you put on a murder mystery for them?

Some of my favorite programs ever have come simply from chatting with my kids about what they want. Teen Advisory has been our source for such information for a long time, but with busier schedules than ever teen groups come and go. In the next chapter I'll give you strategies to obtain that information in a fun new way.

9

◇ ◇ ◇

A NEW TAKE ON TEEN ADVISORY

Teen Advisory is a long-standing tradition in libraries. Hearing directly from our teen patrons on the services they want, collection holes they see, and general changes they want to see made keeps us current. If not for their input we would be trapped in our worlds of book reviews, peer articles, and a hopeful look at pop culture to guess what our patrons are looking for. However, as many teen schedules become busier than ever Teen Advisory groups can find their numbers dwindling and participation spotty.

Engaging today's teens meaningfully means updating the structure of Teen Advisory groups and rewarding them for their participation. Reassess your Teen Advisory Board (TAB) as a volunteer group that is constantly giving you feedback. Rewarding this group with an after-hours celebration will bring them together to give you feedback collectively. Today's teens have schedules that are more jam-packed than ever, but this combination of flexibility and reward gives them more options to help the library when they're available.

STOCKING THE PANTRY

- Large space to run around and be loud in
- Tables
- Chairs
- Scratch paper on each table
- Markers for each table
- Library Bucks to spend (10 per person): use one color for 'tweens and teens and another color for adults

- Sheets of paper on the walls with your questions
- Sheet of paper on the wall with your new program ideas on envelopes for them to spend their money in

Grownups and 'tweens/teens get different colored Library Bucks so that you can track who's interested in what. We've all received feedback from adults on programs the library should offer only to find that when the big day comes no one attends but tumbleweeds. On the other hand, you can also track what programs both kids AND their families are excited about for a real winner!

PROMOTING YOUR PROGRAM

Talking this up with your regulars will be a big help. Let them know that their love for this place can go to the next level, and they can help determine what happens next by attending. They're already hanging out with you because they like what you're doing—why not reward them with the gift of meaningful input?! As an added bonus, your volunteers are likely to attend since immediately following the focus group will be the after-hours celebration.

Make sure you've got a bright poster up that advertises the program and reminds participants that they'll help determine the next big program you'll do. For a lot of people this is the draw of participating.

RECIPES

The Focus Group

A focus group—so long as it's interactive and fun—can be a great way to get some valuable information from your audience. You want to know what they like, what they don't like, and what they want. Honesty, knowing the good and the bad, is what's going to help your department improve.

Once the focus group is over, actually bringing about the changes your patrons would like to see will both empower them and give them ownership over the space. You'll build lifelong fans and teach them a little something about the power of the vote. Run them quarterly so you don't burn your participants out, and you'll have plenty of time to research more fun games to play!

Tab Indicators

STEAM

S:

T:
E: Working together to create change
A: Doodling while listening, writing ideas and feedback
M: Dividing bucks into programs they'll vote for

Time

1 hour

Age level

8- to 18-year-olds (and their families!)

Ingredients

- Tables
- Chairs
- Large sheets of paper
- Tape
- Markers
- Prizes of some sort—small candies, toys, coupons for free rentals, hot chocolate, whatever you've got!
- Volunteer applications
- Pens or pencils
- Library Bucks in two colors

This will be the most fun if you create them yourself to reflect your own culture. Might be a buck with your building featured on it. Might be there's a storm trooper somewhere because your kids are really into *Star Wars*. Make it your own and let the fun fly! For a simple example, check out the Resources section.

Setup

1. First figure out what kind of information you're looking for from this group. Are you looking for programming ideas? Do you want to know which piece of technology they would like purchased? Are you looking for collection development ideas? Want to know if they're interested in your library lending experiences, like kits that teach you how to knit or collage? If you're not totally sure what to ask, here are some great starter questions:
   a. What are we doing well?
   b. What can we do better?
   c. What's your favorite thing about the library?
   d. If you could have anything in the library and money were no option, what would you want?

Question d. is one we take very seriously. People have a tendency to think that making small suggestions is more helpful than making big sweeping ones. However, unless folks are honest, the feedback you receive is no good at all. Encourage them to shoot for the moon and you'll learn more about their culture than you could imagine. We've heard everything from installing a zip line to a coffee bar. Take every request seriously and discuss what each change would be like within the library. We give them what we can and keep asking so we stay in line with what they truly want.

2. Hang up big sheets of paper with your questions written on them and room for answers below.
3. What new programs are you considering running? Create another large sheet of paper with the names of four to six programs written on it and an envelope under each name. Hang this up on the wall also.
4. Set a large piece of paper on each table for people to doodle on and scatter markers around on the tables.
5. Set up a small area for you where you can take notes, keep the prizes, hang on to the extra library bucks, and have the volunteer applications and pens/pencils ready.
6. Finally, if you're feeling brave hang another sheet of large paper on the wall for each librarian that will be participating and your room setup is complete.

Instructions

1. Welcome everyone to the focus group by handing them their 10 library bucks and inviting them to take a seat and doodle. (Don't forget, adults get different colored library bucks!)
2. Thank them for coming and explain that the purpose for the night is to let the library know what it's doing right, where it can improve, and what the participants hope will happen in the future!
3. Go around the room and give everyone a chance to say who they are and their favorite thing about the library. You can jot down these answers on the large piece of paper on which this question appears. Don't make people take a turn if they're clearly shy or uncomfortable speaking in front of a group. In fact, if that happens it's the perfect time to point out the doodle paper they've been drawing on. Let the group know that if there's anything they want to tell you but are uncomfortable saying out loud they can write it on the doodle paper and you'll see it later after everyone has left.
4. When you have everyone's answers recorded, point out the other sheets on the wall with all the questions.
5. Once you've read the questions aloud, ask your participants to please get up and answer as many questions as they can. Let them know that you won't be watching them answer, so all the answers

will be anonymous. When they're finished they can return to their doodle paper. If you're struggling with what to do while they get busy, just head to the doodle paper and get creative!

6. When everyone is back to their doodle paper, head to the first question and read the answers aloud. Encourage folks to raise their hands if what you read is something they agree with. Make tick marks next to the answer to keep track of what's a popular answer and what's not.

7. If you hear an answer you especially love you can throw out some of those small prizes to everyone who agrees with you.

I know what you're thinking: "If I start handing out prizes for folks who agree with me everyone will just raise their hands to get a prize, skewing my results!" Well, you're right. However, if you record your tick marks then hand out prizes you'll have your accurate count. If folks raise their hands after that just to get the prize so be it. You have your count. Just give them a prize, and you can all continue on your merry way.

8. Once you've run through this portion, it's time for folks to spend their hard-earned Library Bucks. Introduce them to the paper on the wall with the envelopes. Give them a brief rundown of your proposed programs and then tell them to use their money to buy any program they want. BUT it doesn't all have to be spent in the same place! Whichever program receives the most money will be the next program you run!

To truly wow your focus group you'll really need to mean what you say. If you say you're going to start running this program next week, you'd better be prepared to do so. Otherwise, you'll lose credibility, and they'll stop coming to give you feedback. This creates some extra work for your plate, but if these are all programs you've already planned out, you should be ready to go anyway. The other programs you won't be using are now created and you can run them as well or save them for another time when they'll be a better fit for your audience.

9. Optional step for those feeling brave! Remember those blank pieces of paper for the librarians participating in the focus group? As participants finish spending their money you can sit in a chair in front of these pieces of paper. Participants can take a marker and write something about you on the piece of paper that they like or don't like about how you're doing at work. It can be funny, brutally honest, and incredibly entertaining—not to mention they make great photos for social media!

10. Finally, thank your participants for all their help and let them know how you'll announce the winner of the new program. Also, let them know that the after party you're about to throw is for your

loyal volunteers. If they'd like to sign up to be a volunteer so they can participate in the next after party they can fill out a volunteer application and give it back to you. No matter when you said you'd post the results, make sure you keep it timely. Don't wait too long and lose their enthusiasm!

11. When it's time to reread your results from the focus groups, look for common things people are asking for and keep track of the kinds of programs the adults are voting for versus what the 'tweens and teens are asking for. Are they the same? Different? Does it leave you with more questions to ask at your next focus groups? Consider who else in your organization should hear the results of these focus groups and report accordingly. Also, save the information for future grant proposals you may write. This is truly valuable information. Don't just toss it!

The After Party

The after party is your chance to reward your volunteers for their hard work! Let them have first dibs at the new video games you're purchasing or the new equipment you got for your department before anyone else gets to try it. Offer up extra games and good snacks, and above all, let them know how grateful you are for all their hard work! Consider bringing in guest stars to lead special classes or programs for them if you have the staff or money to do so.

Tab Indicators

STEAM

- S: Offering a taste of a flashy new science program just for them
- T: Playing with new equipment or tools before anyone else
- E: Providing a fun maker lesson just for them
- A: Offering special arts classes on painting, drawing, crafting, etc. Let them try their hand at your newest piece of art equipment before the general public. Give them free rein in your art supplies for 15 minutes or so
- M: Keeping score during video game tournaments or other games

Time

1 hour

Age level

8 to 18 years

Ingredients

- All your normal toys plus anything new you haven't released to the public yet, like Bedazzlers, Rainbow Looms, your 3D printer, or anything else you've recently purchased
- Food
- Drinks
- Art supplies
- Small prizes—coupons for free cocoa/coffee, movie rentals, etc.

Setup

1. Set out your food and drinks for them to self serve.
2. Decide if you're going to celebrate a specific volunteer, and if so, for what?
   a. Most hours volunteered?
   b. Most programs led?
   c. Most program attendees?

These can change each quarter if you want to.

3. Decide if you want to give away advanced reader copies or let them have first dibs on your newest books. If you do, put those aside so they're ready to go when you decide to release them.
4. Create a special announcement for your Facebook page, Web page, or other social media sites to highlight their accomplishments and sing their praises to the world! Publish it after you announce the featured volunteer!

Instructions

1. Start by playing a high energy game to set the tone for the celebration. Boppity Bop Bop Bop is an all-time favorite! The rules are here: http://www.playworks.org/playbook/games/boppity-bop-bop-bop.
2. As the hour goes by, keep bringing out your newest toys for them to try before the general public does. Explain what you're thinking of doing with the toys, whether it's a new antiprogramming station, an after-school workshop you're designing, or whatever. Get their feedback and pay attention to how they use the equipment. It can lead you to new ideas about how to incorporate them into your programming.
3. You can also give them first dibs on any advance reader copies you may have, or you could save some of the new titles that have come in for them to have first dibs on.
4. Provide some fun all-access micro events:
   a. Give them 15 minutes to create whatever they want using your art supplies. They might be pretty familiar with those supplies from

helping you prep for events, but the opportunity to create something to keep for themselves is awesome and will be a behind-the-scenes indulgence!

5. Play some extra games. Some favorites (with instructions) include
   a. Sardines (http://www.group-games.com/action-games/sardines.html)
   b. Giants, Wizards, Elves (http://www.icebreakers.ws/medium-group/giants-wizards-elves.html)

6. About halfway through the hour is a good time to announce the winning volunteer and present him or her with the designated prize(s). Don't forget to say why this person won the award, whichever quantitative or qualitative measure you chose to measure by.

7. Before your volunteers leave, thank them again for all their hard work and let them know how excited you are to start making the changes they helped you choose.

8. Even if it's informal, be sure to check in with your volunteers and get their opinions on how things are going. It could be as simple as talking with as many as possible for a few seconds each about their opinions on how your volunteer program is going or by asking the group as a whole "By a show of thumbs up or thumbs down, how are we treating our volunteers?" If you need more formal feedback, a simple survey at the end of the night, when kids are about to leave, will give you honest feedback as they'll be leaving and feeling more anonymous than if you were to give it out at the beginning of the night. Some good questions for this more formal survey can include:
   a. What was your favorite volunteer experience with the library since the last after-hours celebration?
   b. What was your favorite volunteer experience at the library ever?
   c. Do you like our method of communicating with you about volunteer stuff?
   d. What could we do better in regards to our volunteer program?

Resources

Great Web resources for icebreakers:

This site is dedicated to icebreakers: http://www.icebreakers.ws/
40 Icebreakers for Small Groups: http://insight.typepad.co.uk/40_icebreakers_for_small_groups.pdf
This site for college resident assistants has lots of games: http://www.residentassistant.com/games/index.htm

2nd Floor Bucks
Good for One Whatever!
Thanks for Helping at this Focus Group.

2nd Floor Bucks
Good for One Whatever!
Thanks for Helping at this Focus Group.

Tips and Tricks

- There are a lot of icebreaker-type games out there for you to choose from when it comes to running your focus group or after party. Go ahead and keep trying new ones until you find the ones you're good at leading and the ones your teens/'tweens/families like participating in. Building an arsenal of these games can get you out of a jam if folks start looking or acting bored or start disrupting the group.
- Playing with the format of your after party is going to happen. It's written loosely here because you really need to stay tuned in to your group and learn to read their cues. You want to keep the energy high but not burn through all your activities and special treats within the first half hour. Play with your timing and learn your audience. Pay attention to them, and they'll tell you what they want—even if they don't say a thing.

I mentioned that movie events are a super fun way to get teens to volunteer at your library, and in the next chapter I'll teach you how to run them, decorate them, and blow your kids' minds with them!

10

◇ ◇ ◇

MOVIE RELEASE EVENTS

The release of a movie based on popular teen fiction or a graphic novel is always a great reason to celebrate! Luckily these days our theaters are rife with titles spawned from such books. Plus, with companies like Marvel announcing well in advance the titles they'll be releasing over the course of upcoming years we have LOTS of time to prepare, no matter how short staffed we are.

While the celebration of a film is super cool for the teens and 'tweens who are already fans of the series or book, it can also open new literary doors to your patrons who may not have read the books yet. In general, an event like this will spawn lots of book talk; make sure to key in on those kids who love the book as they will be your best advocates to sell the title to a new audience. Be sure you're offering a chance for your teens to check out books, even if it's after hours! (*Especially* if it's after hours! How special!) Speaking of which, if at all possible, do this kind of event after your library has closed. It really builds a sense of ownership for your teens, and they can just go bananas and get as loud as they want!

Create the kind of event people would never expect in a library—loud, messy, and interactive—and your movie events will have teens talking about your library long after the doors have closed for the evening. Most importantly, the magic truly lies in the details for events like this—every chance you have to go over the top should be taken. Fanboys and fangirls will love you for it, and it will show everyone you're not just slapping something together but are as excited as they are to celebrate!

Finally, showing movies in your library requires a public performance license, which ensures that these movies are shown legally in public venues. "Under the Copyright Revision Act of 1976 all non-private exhibitors of registered copyrighted videos or DVDs must obtain a Public Performance License. 'Willful' infringement for commercial or financial gain is a federal crime carrying a maximum sentence of up to five years in jail and/or a $250,000 fine." These can be purchased for individual events or for a flat rate can be purchased for one year; the license only covers movies being shown IN the library, not outdoors. Once you have your license you can show any movie covered by that license that you have obtained legally, whether it's from your own collection, the library's collection, or rented.

STOCKING THE PANTRY

Decorating Materials

These will vary based on whatever movie you're celebrating. For example, if you're throwing a party for a Marvel movie you can create a photo booth prop out of cardboard and large paper that looks like a comic book cover; teens can pose behind it and look like they're in a comic book. If you're throwing a Harry Potter party you would want loads of those black plastic cauldrons left over from Halloween. Whatever you're creating, the worksheets in the Resources section will help you prepare.

Activity Materials

Again, the materials you need for each party will vary. If you were going to host that Marvel party you might want to grab some shiny fabric scissors and sticky Velcro to let the teens make their own capes. The worksheet in the Resources section will help you prepare.

Giveaways

The movie you're planning to feature may dictate what you decide to give away, but consider talking to your local movie theater in advance about buying tickets in bulk for the year to hand out as prizes. They may offer you a special rate or even give you extra for free!

You can also contact local businesses and ask if they'd like to sponsor one of these events. If the organization is willing to purchase a set number of movie tickets for you, then in exchange you would include their logo in your publicity and highlight your partnership in any media. Same thing goes if you're giving away DVDs. Ask if stores will offer a discount for purchasing multiple copies or ask local business if they'd like to donate a copy in exchange for sponsorship perks.

Each book or film has its own cool extra details you can offer as giveaways, too. Perhaps a local bakery would be willing to donate a loaf of "Peeta's bread" for your next *Hunger Games* event. You could use the 3D printer to make baby Groods for participants in the next *Guardians of the Galaxy* event. The possibilities are endless!

PROMOTING YOUR PROGRAM

If you have a good volunteer program, signing up your teens to be helpers will help spread the word. If you don't, these events are the perfect opportunities to recruit volunteers who will love you forever. (And then spread the word . . .)

Get yourself a large poster that's eye catching and relevant to the movie. As with any big teen event you'll really want to promote the following: prizes, food, after-hours status. In addition, it's always a good idea to post the movie rating on your poster so parents know what their children will be viewing. Think carefully about where to hang your posters, too. You'll be putting a lot of time and money into this event and need a good crowd to make it worth your while. Ask first and then hang your posters at

- Comic book stores
- Music stores
- Bookstores
- Movie theaters
- Grocery stores
- Schools
- Chamber of Commerce
- Local restaurants
- Recreation centers
- Youth centers
- Churches

In addition to your poster, it's helpful to have a small print flyer (1/4 page) with the details and major selling points available to hand out. They're great reminders and an excellent way for folks who may know someone who's interested to pass along the message in a format you've designed. You can scatter them in high-traffic areas, tuck them into a book at each checkout, and give them to schools to hand out.

Talk to your local middle and high school to see if you can get on the announcements, too. Make sure you promote the wackiest, craziest, larger-than-life part of your event and your prizes, if you have any.

Promoting the event on your social media sites is a must, especially if you can get your teen volunteers to repost it to their pages, feeds, etc.! Your website should have a write-up or event listing. You should create a Facebook event, and you can use Twitter to redirect your followers to your website.

Finally, large, splashy events like this can be a local photographer's dream. If you have press contacts it's time to tell them what you're up to and invite them to come get some great photos!

RECIPES

All great movie events consist of three parts: decorations, activities, and volunteers. The timing of a movie event can be done in two ways.

Party the Night the Movie Comes Out

Celebrate the movie's arrival in theaters by having your party right before release time. This may mean actually doing it one day in advance so your teens can catch the midnight release. If there won't be a midnight release, time your event so your teens can still make it to the first showing.

Party the Night the DVD Comes Out

If the timing doesn't work for a theater release party, you can also celebrate when the DVD is released. If you still have a local video store, talk to the manager and ask to borrow a copy in advance so you can show it promptly at midnight on release day. Unfortunately, with rental places almost nonexistent these days that's hard to come by. However, don't let it deter you. The option of watching the movie while it's attached to a celebration is always enticing to teens, especially if you're able to purchase the copy you watch and then give it away as a prize!

Decorations

Your decorating can range from simple to over the top, but try to reflect the mood or certain features of the film if you can. Recreating the imagery or settings of a book can be difficult and at times downright impossible. How am I supposed to create a massive training center or a Ferris wheel? How can I possibly re-create five different societies in my too small/too large/too quiet/too loud space?!? Don't sweat it! If you have the ability to create a larger-than-life piece of the book, then do it! If not, try to re-create the vibe of the book. Dystopian futures look dark, grungy, scary, and rife with propaganda. There should be visuals to match the look, and music can also help set the mood.

Allow yourself months in advance to prepare your decorations. Starting this early gives you time to use your volunteers and stay flexible with their schedules while ensuring that the work actually gets done. In addition, it will provide you with time to add special details that pop up in your planning and research.

> The larger the space you'll be having your event in, the more decorating you'll need to do. That may sound like a simple concept, but when I moved into Chattanooga's 'tween/teen area, which is over 12,000 square feet, it presented some real challenges. For instance, for a Tim Burton themed area I created I had to use nearly 300 butterflies to re-create a Corpse Bride touch. And that's just ONE of the special touches we wanted for that day. It takes a lot of time, but a team of great teen volunteers can make these tasks easier for you!

In the Resources section there's a worksheet you can use to brainstorm decorating. It's partially filled out to give you ideas and get you started. It will also help you keep track of all the visuals you want to create and approximately how much time you believe you'll need to create them.

Activities

While the decorations set the stage for what participants can expect, it's your activities that really contain the magic. What teens and 'tweens do once they're inside your space can make them feel like they're a part of the story, creating an extension of the book they'll treasure. To make things simpler, break your activities down into four categories: group activities, solo activities, classes, and food.

The activities can be just as labor intensive as decorations when it comes to prepping all the pieces you'll need and getting organized. When the big day comes, be sure you're able to get set up quickly and focus on the last-minute decorating. Another worksheet is available in the Resources section to help you plan what to do and how much time it will take to create.

Group activities

Consider both the tone of the book and the activities the characters participate in. If you were throwing a *Hunger Games* party, you would want to create another dystopian vibe in your activities fraught with suspense, adventure, and tension. While you wouldn't necessarily fill a cornucopia with weapons and have your teens fight to the death, you might consider building a cornucopia and filling it with Nerf guns or, even better, foam bows and arrows! A mass Nerf battle is exactly the kind of activity no one would expect to have in a library, and that makes it even more fun! Larger-than-life scenarios like this are massively popular and should be highlighted in your marketing of the event.

Solo activities

Not everything can be a showstopper, so having less intense activities is important, too. Art projects, crafts, games, and maker stations are all fantastic solo activities to incorporate into your event. These are also perfect for when teens need quieter activities, a rest, or some introvert time.

Obvious character groups within the book make a great place to look for creating activities. Think about the various houses from Hogwarts, nerds versus bullies, the factions in *Divergent*, the rich versus the poor, the different cabins from Camp Olympus, etc. What is the purpose of each group? What do they want? Did the groups perform actions you can replicate and turn into activities or do you need to create activities based off their motives? In *The Hunger Games* we know that District 1 is really into fashion. Without a book-related activity that they performed as a group, you could always host some kind of wacky futuristic fashion game: Who can make the craziest District 1 outfit in 15 minutes with only these garbage bags and tape? If there aren't groups of characters to play off of, look to the story's plotline for inspiration. What challenges did the heroes and villains undergo? For example, Frodo crossed challenging terrain and threw the ring into Mount Doom. Sounds like an awesome chance to create an obstacle course!

Classes/guest stars

These activities are a fun way to bring in fresh perspectives for your teens. Think outside the box and get creative as far as who can be involved and what can be taught. If you were doing a Harry Potter event, you could bring in an herbalist to give a lesson on mixing herbal cold remedies. If you were focusing on one of the Marvel movies, you could bring in a stunt double to teach an action movie trick or a comic book artist to give a drawing lesson. Your community has a bevy of talent and unique perspectives for you to draw on. Take advantage of them!

Food

We all know how important food is to teens, and how essential it is with large events, so combining the two means upping your game and making the food extra special. Especially if your book is heavy on food details (think *Harry Potter*, Roald Dahl's works, *Julie & Julia*, *Teenage Mutant Ninja Turtles*) DO play up the food and go over the top! Create butter beer together! Have a pizza-topping bar! Have a Julia Child one-handed egg-breaking contest! Create a giant peach out of Jell-o and surround it with as many gummy bugs as you can purchase! If you're feeling strapped for food ideas on a particular theme, Pinterest is a great resource. There are dozens of great teachers, librarians, parents, and other educators who are throwing well-documented themed parties and posting their ideas daily.

> You may run into trouble with the wave of popularity dystopian books are receiving these days. So many of the characters in these books are starving! How are you supposed to cater starvation?!? The answer is to keep the food simple but return to your details with the decorating. Add intricate labels to the utensils, cups, plates, bags, or whatever they're eating from.

When all else fails, go with the standard for the movies—popcorn. If you can afford to purchase an old-timey looking popcorn maker, I assure you that you will lovingly wear it into the ground. They're showy, set a tone, smell amazing, and make movie-worthy popcorn quickly. If you can't afford to buy one you could always look into renting one or talk to your local movie theater about purchasing pre-popped popcorn. If all else fails, you can make bags and a microwave available.

Volunteers

There are two types of volunteers for large events: those who help ahead of time with creating the decorations and activities and those who help out at the event. While they're both critical to your event's success, they'll be working at different speeds.

Ahead-of-time volunteers

As previously mentioned, it's vital to engage volunteers early on if possible to achieve maximum impact with your decorations and preparing your activities. Many hands make light work, and this will allow you to continue adding touches to wow your participants.

Ahead-of-time volunteers should be encouraged to create at their own pace. After all, you'll be starting well in advance to ensure that they aren't rushed, which could result in their having a bad time and quitting. The goal is not just to get the work done but to be sure the volunteers have fun getting the work done so they'll volunteer with you again.

After you've filled out your worksheets for planning the activities and decorations, you'll have the framework you need to lead your volunteers. There's a volunteer worksheet available in the Resources section that can also help you get organized.

At-the-event volunteers

Volunteers who come to the event to help you should also be treated well. Be sure you're flexible to their schedules and needs. Invite them to help at the entire event, from setup to breakdown. Be prepared for teens who want to participate but can't come for the entire time. Most likely the event from setup to breakdown will take between four and six hours. This time frame usually works really well for teens who have service requirements they're looking to bang out in a day. You know what works best for your teens, but here are some extra tips:

- Give your regulars first dibs on which activities they would like to help with.
- Rotate volunteers through the various stations so they have an opportunity to party as well.
- If you can, sign up more volunteers than you need so they can take breaks and experience the party even further; maybe have them only work half the party.
- If you can secure prizes, you can either give one to each volunteer or have a drawing at the end of the event as an extra reward.
- If you won't be using the decorations again, invite your volunteers to take them home! It'll cost you nothing since the event is over, and the items will be awesome for decorating their rooms!

Tab Indicators

STEAM

These will vary from event to event based on your movie, but here are a few examples:

S: Experimenting with sourdough bread starters to create an Amity loaf to bake at home for a *Divergent* event
T: Using various sewing equipment to make Marvel character-themed costume pieces
E: Constructing a bow and arrow for a *Hunger Games* event
A: Cooking pizza with a local pizza maker for a *Teenage Mutant Ninja Turtles* event
M: Keeping score during a quidditch match for a *Harry Potter* event

Time

Prep: 20 hours+
Event: 2 hours

Age level

13 to 18 years

Resources list

Copyright Revision Act of 1976: http://www.copyright.gov/title17/
FAQ from MovieLicense: http://library.movlic.com/faq#6
My Pinterest board about Harry Potter events: http://www.pinterest.com/bibliochica/2015-harry-potter/

My Pinterest board about *Divergent* events: http://www.pinterest
.com/bibliochica/divergent-release-party/

The following reproducible worksheets will help you get organized
with decorations, activities, and volunteers. Each worksheet is provided
as a blank and is followed by an example of a filled-out sheet to throw a
Divergent themed party.

DECORATIONS

The Overall Feel of the Book is:

Obvious, Big-Impact Themes You Can Recreate & Amount of Time Needed to Create:

Materials Needed:

Small Details You Can Recreate & Amount of Time Needed to Create:

Materials Needed:

Background Elements & Amount of Time Needed to Create:

Materials Needed:

TOTAL Amount of Time Needed:

DECORATIONS

The Overall Theme, Setting, or Mood of the Book is:

Dystopian Future

Obvious, Big-Impact Themes You Can Recreate & Amount of Time Needed to Create:

Ferris wheel posters (2 hours)
Interactive fear maze (7 hours)

Materials Needed:

Poster-sized paper
Extra printer ink
6 giant boxes (couch and fridge size can be found and usually donated from local moving companies or furniture stores)
Random sensory materials to crawl through, over, and under inside the dark maze (crunchy Styrofoam cups, sticky double-sided tape, fluttery streamers, fuzzy yarn, etc.)
12 oversized garbage bags to link the boxes together
Box cutter to manipulate boxes and build
10 rolls duct tape to connect boxes

Small Details You Can Recreate & Amount of Time Needed to Create:

Propaganda posters for each faction (3 hours)

Materials Needed:

Poster-sized paper
Extra printer ink

Background Elements & Amount of Time Needed to Create:

Futuristic space garbage
Ripped trash bags hung all over the place (6 hours)
Caution tape hung around (2 hours)

Materials Needed:

3 rolls of caution tape
24 oversized trash bags

TOTAL Amount of Time Needed:

20 hours

Activities

Groups Within the Book:

Group Activities

Materials Needed:

Solo Activities

By Group

Materials Needed:

Classes/Guest Stars:

Materials Needed:

Food:

Activities

Groups Within the Book:

Dauntless
Amity
Candor
Abnegation
Erudite
Factionless
Divergent

Group Activities

Being sorted into factions with the fear maze

Materials Needed:

Faction buttons to give people as they emerge from the maze:
Erudite
Candor
Dauntless
Abnegation
Amity
Factionless (In case they don't make it through the maze or break the maze)
Blue drink to give teens before they enter the maze
Small cups for the drink

Solo Activities

By Faction

Amity: Make popcorn for participants

Dauntless: Man the building-jump photo booth, tattoo station

Erudite: Secretly in charge of the fear maze and sending participants through again!

Candor: Positive honesty activity (Sit in front of a blank sheet of paper; people write what they like about you behind you. When everyone's gone, peek!)

Abnegation: No mirror makeup challenge (Make yourself pretty without a mirror, then see how you did after!) and use metal-stamping equipment to make a watch-sized piece of jewelry.

Materials Needed:

Popcorn machine
Popcorn supplies
Popcorn bags
Amity labels for popcorn bags
iPad with Green Screen app
White wall for background
Stool to pose on
Temporary tattoos
Large sheets of white paper to sit in front of
Seats
Markers
Makeup
Mirror
Metal washers
Metal-stamping kit
Yarn

Classes/Guest Stars:

Tattoo artist to talk about origins of tribal art
Hair stylist demonstration on how to create a faux hawk
Makeup artist giving out *Divergent* makeovers

Materials Needed:

Water and snacks for guest stars
Thank-you notes for guest stars
Special equipment? (Ask guest stars what you should supply)

Food:

Popcorn
Blue juice at entrance of maze

Volunteers

Ahead of Time

For Decorations & Amount of Time Needed:

For Activities & Amount of Time Needed:

At the Event & Amount of Time Needed:

Setup:

Activities & Amount of Time Needed:

Breakdown:

Volunteers

Ahead of Time

For Decorations & Amount of Time Needed:

Tear-apart trash bags (10–15 hours)
Cut white edges off posters (2–3 hours)

For Activities & Amount of Time Needed:

Cut large white pieces of paper to hang behind participant's heads (½ hour)
Cut lengths of ribbon/yarn for washer metal-stamping bracelets (½ hour)
Cut apart temporary tattoos (½ hour)
Create Amity labels for popcorn bags (2 hours)
Paste Amity labels onto popcorn bags (1 hour)

At the Event & Amount of Time Needed:

Setup:

Hang propaganda posters (½ hour)
Decorate with caution tape (45 minutes)
Set up food area with popcorn machine plugged in and bags on top (20 minutes)

Activities & Amount of Time Needed:

Erudite:
Lead the fear maze activity (1–2 hours)

Candor:
Lead honesty activity (1–2 hours)

Divergent:
Lead the photo booth activity (1–2 hours)
Give tattoos (1–2 hours)

Amity:
Make and hand out popcorn (1–2 hours)

Abnegation:
Lead makeup activity (1–2 hours)
Lead metal-stamping activity (1–2 hours)

Breakdown:

Invite all volunteers to take a piece of your decorations home with them!
Take down all paper decorations and the tape holding them up; recycle
Clean up food area
Sweep for random debris (cups, popcorn bags, other trash) and throw away
Pick up activities and place them in designated areas

From *Cooking Up Library Programs Teens and 'Tweens Will Love: Recipes for Success* by Megan Emery Schadlich. Santa Barbara, CA: Libraries Unlimited. Copyright © 2015.

Tips and Tricks

- A poster is a necessary visual for promoting these events, but you'll really want to talk the event up yourself. Word of mouth truly is the best advertising. As your event gets closer, you'll want to engage every teen, 'tween, or known parent of a 'tween or teen in a conversation about whether they've heard of the event yet—and get one of your ¼-page flyers into their hands.

- When it comes to breaking down your event, you may have teens who are super into it and want to stay until the bitter end, offering you their blood, sweat, and tears because they love you and the library so much. They will make your life infinitely easier, and you will cherish them. On the other hand, you may have a room full of teens who can't wait to get out of there and want nothing to do with cleaning up. Recognize that both are totally acceptable and that cleanup is a part of your job. You're lucky if they'll help out, but if not, who cares! Let them be teens and get back to work!

Putting together large events like this is a lot of fun and can be addictive. If you're like me and you love the challenge of making these show stoppers, then you'll love the next chapter. It's the ultimate in large events specifically for teens highlighting the best of the best for what's available to them specifically in your community.

11

❖ ❖ ❖

TEEN OPPORTUNITIES FAIR

Now more than ever unemployment and underemployment are problems for our newest entrants into the job market. When it comes to transitioning into the professional world many of our communities have resources available for teens and new adults that they don't even know about or that have been traditionally viewed as suitable for professionals already in the workforce. Like libraries or schools, many nonprofits have little to no marketing budgets and are facing the same advertising problems that libraries face. This is where the Teen Opportunities Fair comes in. It is a hands-on showcase of what's available locally for teens, ages 14 to 19 years, in the following five areas:

- Volunteer opportunities
  - Who is creating high-quality volunteer experiences that translate into job and scholarship applications, not simply having teens stuff envelopes and answer phones? These agencies are eager to advertise what they have available and walk teens through the application process on the spot at the fair.
- Internship opportunities
  - Paid or unpaid, an internship looks great when it comes to taking your next step professionally. Who in your area has internships available to teens or young adults just starting out in the workforce? Representatives will be happy to come and advertise these internships and assist teens in filling out applications on the spot.
- Employment opportunities
  - Most teens will come to the fair wanting (or even expecting) to get hired on the spot. This is a great setting for your local businesses

and organizations who hire teens to let them know what their jobs entail and to walk them through the application process at their table. Having employers at the fair also teaches teens that hiring does not happen as it does in the movies but instead takes patience, thought, and even planning.

- Continuing education opportunities
  - ○ Colleges and universities are a natural fit for the fair, but think big. Students who aren't ready to commit to college can at least stay professionally viable and a serious candidate by taking a class or continuing their education in a subject they think they're interested in pursuing professionally. Adult education centers, educational cooperatives, or professional/management training centers are all great resources to check.
- Professional development opportunities
  - ○ Opening a checking account, dressing professionally, or using e-mail are serious forms of communication that can be a mystery to some teens. Consider the racial, sexual, financial, political, and historical makeup that pepper your communities' culture. Now factor in the millennial generation's need for instant feedback and fast turnaround. Many of the things older generations learned in school or through the excitement of that newfangled Internet simply aren't commonplace for our teens. Professional development is a serious opportunity to bridge some gaps. Local nonprofit organizations, such as Dress for Success, Financial Education Centers, and more, can promote the programs they offer for new professionals while offering onsite advice and examples of how to immediately make changes in a teen's professional outlook.

By highlighting what's happening locally for your teens and young adults, you can help transition them into the next chapters of their lives while building fruitful community partnerships with other local organizations. You will show your youth that your community values them, and you will show your community that your youth have professional ambitions that are to be taken seriously.

Working with professional development organizations at an opportunity fair can evolve into those organizations collaborating with the library to offer classes on topics like creating a professional e-mail address or applying for a job online (and following up!). This takes the job fair model and transitions it into a conference model.

STOCKING THE PANTRY

- Food
  - ○ Remember, you're highlighting what's special locally at this fair. If you have a budget that allows you to afford to purchase food,

do so locally and let another business in to shine. The business can cater the event and even do some of its own recruiting if it's looking to hire. If you don't have a budget for this, consider applying for local funding to purchase food. It's one more way to build relationships based on supporting one another instead of receiving donations. Everyone is looking for donations, so set yourself apart by being a small business supporter, if you can!

- If the event is not catered, offer fair attendees a ticket when they enter to redeem for one of the following:
  - Snack:
    - Bag of pretzels
    - Apple
    - Small bottled juice/water
    - Local favorite
      - Handmade chocolate
      - Roll from a local bakery
      - Locally grown fruit
  - Lunch:
    - Cheese pizza or garden salad
    - Soft drinks or bottled juice/water
    - Local favorites
      - Sambusa
      - Whoopie pies
      - Corn fritters
      - What's special in *your* area?
  - Locate local donations of food or funding for food.
    - Always provide advertising sponsorships to financial or in-kind supporters on your promotional materials and be sure to mention their names during the event or to the media when you get coverage.
    - Reach out to
      - Local organizations
        - Lions Club
        - Rotary
      - Local food providers
        - Farmer's market
        - Local restaurant
        - Supermarket
- Door prizes
  - Offer local agencies and businesses a free table at the event in exchange for door prizes.
  - Work with them to make sure you wind up with prizes the teens will respond well to. Gift cards work best, especially for things like
    - Downloadable music/games/books
    - Movie tickets

- Pizza
- Sandwich shops
- Video games
- Music stores

Remember, you're highlighting what's great locally, so encourage tabling organizations to use their own products or shop locally!

Gift cards can also be purchased if you have the budget for it or you can reach out to local businesses and see if they'd like to donate. But remember, everyone is asking for donations, so, if possible, be the organization that comes to them excited to purchase and show off their product rather than give it away for free. Building this goodwill may result in donations or sponsorships down the line for you and your organization.

PROMOTING YOUR PROGRAM

This program deserves a solid marketing effort to do the most good. Teens are constantly being recruited to attend fairs and events at this time in their lives, and at times it's even mandatory that they attend. What can make your fair stand apart are three features:

- Great free food
- The possibility that they might get hired (read: $$$)
- Door prizes they're interested in

Don't be afraid to play up those three appeals and let the other awesome local organizations reap the benefits!

Here are some strategies:

- Get the fair listed on school announcements. Usually schools ask for a write-up or a quick blurb. Don't be afraid to be funny or to push those three big sellers: food, jobs, and prizes.
- Create a large and eye-catching poster. If you have a graphic designer to shop this out to, don't hesitate. If not, consider including this in any funding requests you're writing or presenting. Teens are already under a constant barrage of professionally designed marketing materials and, as such, have a very low tolerance for what typically passes as library marketing material. Put up your posters anywhere the teens are:
  - Schools
  - Rec centers
  - Concert venues
  - Local colleges

- ○ Skate parks
- ○ Churches
- ○ Restaurants
- ○ Supermarkets
- ○ Movie theaters
- ○ Participating agencies' locations
- ○ Anywhere you're purchasing prizes or food for the fair!
- Speak at local organizations about what you're creating:
  - ○ Rotary
  - ○ 1,000,000 Cups (http://www.1millioncups.com/)
  - ○ United Way
  - ○ Volunteer administrator groups
  - ○ Chamber of Commerce
  - ○ Lions Club
  - ○ Job fairs

RECIPES

Teen Opportunities Fair

There are three distinct components to the fair:

- Exhibits area
- Classes
- Food

The exhibits area is where your visiting organizations display their information and meet with teens one on one. Consider arranging the area in five sections (volunteer, internship, employment, continuing education, and professional training) and allow teens to wander about networking, learning about, and applying for various opportunities.

The classes area is where you'll host short seminars related to those five areas led by people from those organizations, your staff members, and even local teens.

The food area is something that is flexible and can change from venue to venue based on your space, staffing, and population.

Tab Indicators

STEAM

S: Inviting science-based industries like hospitals with internships, research centers offering jobs, and colleges with classes or degrees in the sciences will fill science needs for the fair

T: Inviting local tech-based industries or schools that are hiring, offering internships, or offer continuing education for teens as well as volunteer opportunities will bring a technology focus to your fair

E: Inviting a variety of engineering-based manufacturers and employers like makerspaces, colleges with engineering degrees or classes, or internship opportunities will meet the engineering criteria

A: Inviting art organizations like galleries with internships, schools offering art degrees and classes, or art walks with volunteer opportunities will fulfill this artistic focus

M: Inviting banks that offer checking accounts specifically for teens, professional development organizations that will discuss how to start building credit safely, or mathematical internships and continuing education will benefit this area

Your fair will vary in these areas, but using STEAM as a framework will help you keep a balanced offering for your teens.

Time

2 to 5 hours

Age level

14 to 19 years

Ingredients

- Tables
- Chairs
- In-house signage for teens/families
- In-house signage for organizations
- Flyers with schedule, class locations, sponsors
- Food, coffee, tea, and hot water for organizations, and teachers/presenters

Setup

1. Determine how much room you have
   - Exhibits area
     - How many tables can you fit in your space?
     - If you divide that number by five how many representatives can you host for each of the five areas of opportunity?
   - Classes
     - How many spaces do you have to host classes? Do you have classrooms or will you be using dividers? Are you limited by other classes that are offered in those spaces?

- What are your dream classes?
  - Some ideas:
    - Applying for jobs online
    - Travel the country with AmeriCorps
    - Etsy crash course
    - Interview like a boss
    - Networking (face to face, not online)
    - Build your resumé with quality volunteer experiences
    - An onsite service activity for a local organization
      - Creating cards for military troops or a local retirement community
      - Assembling craft packets for a local day care center
      - Try to keep things fresh though—no stuffing envelopes or cutting stuff out, if possible. You want to impress the teens, not bore them.
  - Can your attending organizations teach teens new skills?
  - Do they have their own specialties to teach?
  - How long should classes be?

2. Recruit local organizations
   - Start planning 6 to 8 months in advance to give enough lead time. Remember, the organizations you're contacting also have to ask permission and run things past their own boards before moving forward.
   - Send e-mail No. 1 (a sample appears at the end of the chapter) to potential organizations.
   - Remember, you want organizations that teens are already into and organizations they may not have heard of that can open their eyes to what's available to them locally. Here are examples for each of the five categories:
     - Internships
       - Local nonprofits, especially those with heavy summer or evening programming like art walks, summer concert series, marathons, etc.
       - Recreation centers
       - Colleges
     - Volunteer
       - Humane societies
       - Food shelters
       - Art walks
       - Goodwill Industries
       - Land trusts
       - Time banks

- ○ Employment
  - ▪ Any large organizations that historically hire teens (think fast-food chains, coffee shops, shopping centers, grocery stores, etc.)
  - ▪ Recreation centers
  - ▪ Goodwill Industries
  - ▪ AmeriCorps
  - ▪ Boys & Girls Clubs
  - ▪ Military recruitment offices
- ○ Professional development
  - ▪ Girls Inc.
  - ▪ Banks or credit unions
  - ▪ ROTC
  - ▪ Dress for Success
- ○ Continuing education
  - ▪ Universities
  - ▪ Colleges
  - ▪ Adult education centers
  - ▪ Makerspaces
  - ▪ Cooperatives (arts, volunteer, housing)
  - ▪ Schools that offer year-long postgraduate programs
3. Recruit volunteers: Getting teens to help run the fair will both help your case for empowering your local youth and will spread the word about their fair to their families and friends.
   - Determine what volunteer opportunities you'll have available, such as food servers, table runners (to provide bathroom breaks, get water, etc.), people responsible for setup and breakdown, greeters (to pass out food tickets and flyers), and class guides (to spread the word about and lead teens to classes).
   - If you have a regular pool of volunteers, pull from there and offer them first dibs on the jobs to show your appreciation to them for their continued service.
   - To recruit new volunteers, talk up your unique volunteer opportunities specific to the fair in advance as you're presenting to community groups. Talk to your regular teen patrons, get their opinions on the fair, and ask if they'd like to get involved. Have volunteer applications and a flyer with the information about helping at the fair at the ready at all times so you can recruit in a split second!
   - Purchase and reserve some special prizes just for your volunteers. This is a big event with a lot of working parts, and their assistance will make it even better. Show them how much you appreciate them by purchasing gift cards (or asking some of the participating

businesses to donate them). If you don't have the money for that, take a look at something specific to your organization. For example: does your library have $1 movie rentals or an ongoing book sale? Give them coupons for free goodies!

4. Food: Depending on your space and time line, there are two simple and cost-effective ways to handle this. However, you know your space better than anyone else and should talk over with your staff what will be the most convenient for everyone involved.
   - As participants enter the fair, hand out snack/lunch bags that you've assembled with local goodies ahead of time.
   - Give tickets they turn in at a designated area for snack/lunch.

Instructions

The day of the fair will look something like this:

1. You arrive one or two hours before setup to make sure the space is ready for setup. If you're offering coffee, tea, or refreshments for volunteers get them set up now.
2. Welcome your volunteers 30 minutes before exhibitors arrive, thank them again, and get them plugged into their tasks (setting out sack lunches, getting trash cans positioned for convenience, assisting tabling vendors with their own set up, etc.).
3. Help your organizations get set up at their tables for the remaining hour before the fair opens to the public.
4. Open the doors to the teens, and enjoy!
5. Stick to your schedule, and keep everyone pumped up about the offerings you've curated for the teens. Keep moving. Check in with organizations at tables as well as with teens, and get qualitative feedback.

After the fair will look something like this:

1. You should have e-mail addresses for all participating organizations. Send out an online survey to get feedback on what went well, what can be improved, and any other input your participating organizations may have.
2. When you know the date of the next Teen Opportunities Fair, send it out right away to get participants signed up. Keep in mind that not everyone who participated may be the right fit for this fair. There's no obligation to keep the exact same organizations there year after year. In fact, that could get monotonous to the teens.

Resources

Sample e-mail No. 1:

Greetings (contact's name),

(your name) from (your organization) here. We met at _____ /
I was given your contact information from _____ , and
I'm writing to let you know about an exciting opportunity for (your organization): The Teen Opportunities Fair. The Teen Opportunities Fair will
showcase the best local organizations and business for teens in five distinct areas:

1. Internships
2. Volunteering
3. Employment
4. Continuing education
5. Professional development

With underemployment and unemployment skyrocketing for teens
these days, our community has a unique challenge to give our kids a
competitive edge. By working together with us, (your organization) has
decided to be proactive in giving our youth the advantages they need.
The Teen Opportunities Fair is one part exhibits opportunity for our local
businesses to meet and network with some of our young citizens; and
one part convention, where our teens can learn about just how much is
offered locally to assist them in entering the job market in a casual and
instructional setting.

I hope (organization you're contacting) will consider participating in
the _____ area of the fair because of the services you offer. (Give
examples of their programs or services you particularly think would be a
good fit for the fair. Also, if you have any anecdotes from teens speaking to
their being a need for the kind of services the organization offers include
those here. For example: I see ArtWalk fitting into our volunteer area perfectly because of the unique volunteer opportunities you've created. Many
teens are interested in the arts but seem to lose that part of their lives once
they enter the professional world. Participating in an arena of our community where professional artists mix with others who simply maintain
their artistic endeavors on the side offers a valuable life lesson. It can show
teens that their artistic talents have monetary value and that even if they
don't pursue a career in the arts, it can stay a part of them throughout life.
Volunteering with ArtWalk can give our teens that exposure and potentially alter their lives. We would love to have you participate!)

Exhibiting at the Teen Opportunities Fair is free. We simply ask that you donate a door prize. Gift cards for coffee and ice cream shops, movie tickets, museum passes, pizza, or music are always good choices; and we encourage you to shop locally if possible as this fair is intended to highlight all the wonderful businesses and organizations that make our community so special!

The fair is scheduled to take place on (day/month) from (time–time). We will have setup available the day before the fair for your convenience from (time–time).

If you're interested please let me know by (date; a month away is good to get the ball rolling. Wait too long and you could be scrambling to fill empty spots, too soon and you'll lose some potentially great folks by being demanding. You'll be sending out a follow-up e-mail later so a month is flexible yet timely.), and I'll send more detailed information regarding parking (and validation if that's something you do). I'll also want to obtain your logo for our promotional materials.

In addition, if you have a class or presentation you'd be interested in giving at the fair, we will have (#) spots for presentations available; and we will be curating a wide cross-section of topics for our local youth. If you're interested in offering a class, simply let me know your topic, send a brief overview of it in your response to this e-mail, and we'll go from there.

Thanks so much for your time, I look forward to hearing from you!

(Your name)
(E-mail signature)

Sample follow-up to e-mail No. 1 if you've received no response:

Hi (contact's name),

I'm just checking in to see if you've given any thought to my last e-mail about (their organization) participating in (your organization)'s Teen Opportunities Fair.

I know how hectic all of our schedules are these days and don't mean to pressure, but we're eager to finalize the pieces of this stage of the event. We'd still love to have you participate if it fits in with all the great work you're doing.

Please let me know what you think and have a great day!

(Your name)
(E-mail signature)

Sample e-mail No. 2:

Hello (contact's name),

Thanks for your interest in having a table at the Teen Opportunities Fair we're hosting on (date) here at (your organization).

As promised, here's some follow-up information to flesh out the details for you!

1. *Parking*: (Where should people park for set up? Will they need to move their cars to another location after setting up for the duration of the fair? Will they be able to get their cars close again after the fair to break down? Do you validate?)
2. *Setup*: (Where do they park to set up again? Will they be on the ground floor or will they need to take an elevator? Which door should they plan to come in through? Will you have an extra day reserved before for advanced setup to make it easier on their schedules? What is the earliest time they can arrive to set up—on each day if there are two?)
3. *Table Assignment*: (Will organizations be assigned tables by you, or will they simply need to show up and set up in their assigned zone on a first-come, first-served basis?)
4. *Electricity*: (How are you set up when it comes to electrical outlets? Is there one at every spot where there will be a table or not? If not, will you be providing extension cords and power strips or should they plan to bring their own?)
5. *Timeline of the Fair*: (If you have classes in place already, let exhibitors know. Otherwise, let them know what time the doors open to the teens and their families, what time lunch will be served [and that there will be lunch for them!], what time the table portion will end, and what time door prizes will be given. Also, let them know if there will be any special presentation within the exhibits area.)
6. *Door Prizes*: (Remind them about the door prizes and encourage them to call you if they need inspiration or want to bounce an idea off of you. Also, if they would like to drop off their door prize in advance let them know the best way to do that.)

This is shaping up to be an incredible event, and we're thrilled you'll be participating. As I mentioned before, if you have any classes you're interested in teaching at the event, please don't hesitate to let me know. We'll be weighing our options and making our final decisions on all classes and presentations by (date), and we look forward to bringing all this talent to our teens!

You are what makes our community so great to live, work, and play in!

(Your name)
(E-mail signature)

Flyer Sample (Front)

Chattanooga Public Library

Teen Opportunities Fair

Saturday, May 23, 2014

11 am to 2 pm

Timeline

11:00 Doors open: Grab your meal ticket and explore the auditorium

11:30 Class: Applying for Jobs Online & Following Up Like a Boss (Classroom 1)

12:00 Lunch is served in auditorium

12:30 Class: Travel the Country (& Get PAID to Do It!) with AmeriCorps (Classroom 2)

1:15 Class: The Ultimate Vacation: Why Start Saving for Retirement Now? (Classroom 3)

2:00 Door prizes are drawn in the auditorium

From *Cooking Up Library Programs Teens and 'Tweens Will Love: Recipes for Success* by Megan Emery Schadlich. Santa Barbara, CA: Libraries Unlimited. Copyright © 2015.

Flyer Sample (Back)

Locations

- Local businesses, organizations, and nonprofits located in auditorium on the 1st floor

- Classes held on 2nd floor in classroom 1-3

- Lunch served in auditorium on the 1st floor

- Elevators and stairs are located by the circulation desk on the 1st floor

The 2015 Teen Opportunities Fair Is Generously Sponsored by:

From *Cooking Up Library Programs Teens and 'Tweens Will Love: Recipes for Success* by Megan Emery Schadlich. Santa Barbara, CA: Libraries Unlimited. Copyright © 2015.

Tips and Tricks

Bite Off What You Can Chew

The first year I did this it was purely exhibits. Many organizations couldn't fully fathom the potential for something like this, and it was a great way to start by giving both the participating organizations and the teens a positive experience. Everyone raved about the caliber of the interactions they had with the teens and their families; and I built off that success to get folks to put the next year's fair in their calendars right away. Then, after a few months, the idea of classes was introduced to a few compatible organizations and the new, improved Teen Opportunities Fair was born.

Your community may need a similar introductory slice of what this work looks like before they're willing to commit to the whole shebang. We all want to do as much good as possible, but sometimes that means tending our gardens well and letting success come organically.

This fair is a large undertaking with a lot of planning involved, that much is clear. Preparing well in advance is the key to a lot of good programming. If you've got the hang of working this way then you'll love the next chapter. You'll design and run a cool maker camp in a traditional medium that's experiencing a huge resurgence in popularity—the sewing machine!

12

◇ ◇ ◇

SEWING MACHINE CAMP

A lot of great programming within libraries these days has to do with getting kids who are typically engaged in solo hobbies introduced to one another and engaged in a new way. From video games to books themselves, it's easy to get absorbed in your own little world and lose track of everything else. The trick is finding a way to make these interactive, engaging, and catalysts for so much more.

Sewing is a great example of a hobby that historically has only attracted groups of older people for sewing circles, quilting circles, etc. But with the cool resurgence in DIY there is a younger generation chomping at the bit to give sewing a try.

From a maker perspective sewing is a natural fit. You're creating objects by hand, using machinery, technology, experimentation, and more! It's a STEAM dream!

STOCKING THE PANTRY

Sewing Machines

If you're able to purchase these I recommend getting heavy-duty machines that can withstand a variety of fabrics in varying thicknesses and the learning curve battering of your 'tweens and teens. Consider a grant for this program because, as I mentioned before, it's a perfect STEAM activity. You'll want one machine per person, but in a pinch, two kids can share a machine.

Another alternative is to encourage your 'tweens and teens to bring in their own machine—but be careful, you never know what kind of condition they'll be in or if they'll have manuals to go with them. If you're adept at sewing or can invite a team of pros in to help, this may not be a big deal, but you can absolutely expect it to take extra time if not.

A Team of Pros!

Local sewing experts who can give advice on sewing machine repair, maintenance, general use, and techniques will be invaluable to you. Consider looking to your fellow staff members, local Etsy team, sewing or fabric shops, craft societies, and beyond!

Fabric

A random variety is fine for what you'll be teaching, but you do want to be able to have the kids try different kinds and make mistakes. This will absolutely include "fancy" fabrics like tulle, crepes, silks, satins, and those amazing/gaudy rhinestone-covered things. You can purchase a variety of fabric for relatively little money, especially if you check the sale or remnants sections of your local fabric stores or find some clothes to up-cycle from a local thrift store. Another option is to ask for donations from your patrons. You'd be surprised what they have lying around that they'd love to have go to good use!

Thread

Again, a variety will do. You don't have to worry a ton about colors because this is an introductory class—you want your kids to be able to see their stitches. I even recommend starting with a bobbin thread that is a different color from your top thread to make it even easier on your kids. Again, you can ask for donations. Everyone who sews has rolls of thread lying around that they'll never use again!

T-Shirts

I like to ask my kids to bring in their own T-shirts for these classes since they'll leave with an up-cycled item that means even more to them. However, you can always pick some up at a thrift store or ask for clean donations in good shape from your patrons.

> Keep in mind that if you have 'tweens or tiny teens coming to your camp they'll bring small T-shirts. For some projects this is fine, but for others you may need adult-sized shirts. Don't forget to distinguish!

Seam Rippers

These are inexpensive and can be picked up at any sewing store, most fabric stores, and online. You'll want one per person.

Scissors

If you're able, I highly recommend that you get new fabric scissors for this. There's nothing more frustrating than dull scissors when it comes to sewing, especially since it's the first part of the process for most projects. You don't want your group grumpy right out of the gates! You'll want one per person.

Cloth Measuring Tapes

Measuring tapes are inexpensive and can be picked up at any fabric or sewing store or online. You'll want one per person.

Canned Air Dusters

These can be found in hardware stores, sewing stores, and box stores. Usually you can pick up a pack of four, which should be enough. Let your campers share.

> Canned air is catnip for kids. They will laugh, squeal, point it at one another, and use it all up immediately unless you intervene. If you're not great at setting boundaries, you may want to buy extra and keep it hidden until your first batch is depleted.

Sewing Machine Screwdrivers

Sets are inexpensive and can be found at sewing supply stores or fabric stores. Your campers can share, but you'll probably want three or four sets to be safe.

Cups

Paper and plastic cups of any size or shape will do. You can even use lids to jars, small boxes, whatever. These are just to hold screws when machines are taken apart.

Sewing Machine Oil

Bottles are inexpensive and can be found at any sewing supply store or online. Typically, a 4-oz. bottle will last quite a while. Purchase enough for every two campers to share and you'll be in good shape.

PROMOTING YOUR PROGRAM

If you, another staff member, a volunteer, or a neighbor who owes you a big favor have any sewing, needlepoint, or DIY ability, NOW is the time to take advantage of it. A sewn, needlepointed, or handmade poster to promote your program will definitely get people stopping and looking at your bulletin board. You'll want to advertise this camp for four to six weeks in advance to ensure that you get a good turnout.

RECIPES

Threading, Tension, and Anatomy and Care of a Sewing Machine

This first lesson is to familiarize your students with their sewing machines. Everyone wants to jump right in and create something, but unless you teach them the anatomy of their machines and the basics of how they operate, you can plan to spend your entire camp rethreading machines, untangling stitches, and watching your class size dwindle as their frustrations rise. This lesson will get their machines clean, oiled, and familiar. At the end of the lesson, completing a simple sewing project will be rewarding enough to leave them wanting more!

Tab Indicators

STEAM

S: Experimenting with equipment and tools for desired outcomes, hypothesizing solutions to sewing problems
T: Opening and analyzing a sewing machine, using a sewing machine
E: Using tools, cleaning equipment, adjusting equipment, manipulating equipment manually, learning mechanisms of equipment, learning and performing maintenance of equipment
A:
M: Analyzing tension number settings

Time

2 hours

Age level

10 to 18 years

Ingredients

- Tables
- Chairs (one per person)
- Sewing machine for you to use

- Sewing machines for campers to use
- Thread
- Seam rippers
- Sewing machine screwdrivers
- Canned air
- Machine sewing needles
- Scissors
- Cups (one per person to keep screws in)
- Sewing machine oil
- Computer with Internet access
- Fabric (nothing special, just to practice on and soak up oil)

Setup

- Before camp even starts you'll want folks to register to attend. This will allow you to limit your class size to a number you're comfortable with. Give them plenty of time to figure out if camp is going to be a good fit for their own schedules and for yourself to analyze your participants and decide who will be the best fit for what you've created. Your registration criteria are up to you but can include questions like these:
  - Do you have your own machine?
  - Do you have your machine's manual?
  - Have you ever sewn before?
  - How old are you?
  - Are you able to attend all camp sessions?
  - Why do you want to attend Sewing Machine Camp?
- Once registration is complete and you've chosen your campers, you'll want to send out an e-mail letting campers know what to bring with them on the first day. (Find a sample e-mail in the Resources section.)
- Set up a main table where you'll have your machine and equipment ready to show demonstrations. This should be in the front of the room and have plenty of space around it for campers to stand and observe your lessons.
- Spread out your scissors, seam rippers, screwdrivers, cups, sewing machine oil, and thread among the tables. (But keep your canned air at your table!)
- If you have a panel of experts coming they should arrive about 15 minutes before camp starts so you can thank them for coming, offer them some water, and show them where your restrooms are.

Instructions

1. Welcome everyone as they arrive and invite them to have a seat at one of the tables.

2. Once everyone has arrived, ask campers to go around and introduce themselves and share their level of sewing expertise. That
   might be how comfortable they are with sewing, if they've ever
   sewn before, or their favorite project that they've completed.
3. Explain that this camp is all about getting them started with sewing, not making them an expert. Today they'll get started by getting
   to know their machines from the inside out.
4. Introduce your panel of experts (if you have them) and explain that
   these lovely folks will be wandering around offering their help and
   advice today. Tell the teens that if they ever feel lost, to raise a hand
   and someone will come assist them as soon as possible.
5. Threading and tension can be the most frustrating parts of sewing
   and as such is the perfect place to start demystifying sewing. Have
   campers join you at your main table where your machine is set up.
   Run them through your own tension settings and explain that for
   a seam to look even with stitches that are evenly spaced the thread
   needs to travel through the machine at the same rate.

This is a great time to refer to the article on tension from *Threads* magazine that's
referenced in the Resources section.

6. Have everyone pull out their sewing machine manuals. Inside they
   should find the contents and look for a section referring to tension.
   This area should tell them their machine's default setting for tension. If they can't find it, you have your computer to do an Internet
   search for the information. Don't worry if this part takes a while. It
   truly is one of the hardest hurdles to cross when learning to sew. If
   folks finish early you can always start the next step in rounds.
7. Once everyone has set the tension, it's time to return to your main
   table. It's time to show them how to wind a bobbin on your machine.
   Go through the steps and explain that they'll be using two different
   colors for their thread today so they can clearly see the difference
   between their top and bottom threads. Once your bobbin is wound
   show them how you load the bobbin. Have them return to their
   machines and manuals to wind and load their own bobbins.

While it's a good idea to use two different colors of thread for this activity, it's not
a good idea to use threads that are very different in substance. For example, mixing
a thin cotton thread with a heavy-duty quilting thread will create problems. Try and
stick to similar thread types when choosing different colors. That may mean dividing
your threads into different baskets and having campers choose two from the same
basket, or you may want to take the time to discuss the differences and have campers hunt down two similar threads.

8. When their bobbins are ready to go, have the teens rejoin you up front to watch you thread your machine. Most machines will have a graphic on the front that helps explain the order of operations, but it's also useful to check their manuals for instructions. When your machine is threaded, have them return to their machines and manuals to thread their own.

9. Have everyone come up to your main table and then demonstrate taking off the casing of your sewing machine. Once the casing is off show how the parts inside your machine move by manually turning the wheel on the side of your machine.

10. Let everyone go back to their machines, locate the screws to remove the machine's front panel, and then do so! Encourage them to keep their screws in the cups on their tables so they don't roll away or get lost.

11. Once the screws are out and in cups, campers can get up and offer to help others.

12. When all screws are out, have everyone come back to the main table, where you will demonstrate using the canned air to clean out the inside of your machine. Show trouble spots where lots of dust collects in your machine and let them know dust may collect in different spots in their own machines. Explain that machines really only need to be dusted every now and then, not each time you sew.

This is the time to lay down any "No spraying one another" or "Canned air is ONLY to be sprayed inside your machines" type of rules you think would be helpful.

13. Hand out the canned air and let them dust their machines. Let them watch other machines being dusted as a way to see how other machines collect dust differently than their own. When they've dusted their machine they should join you back at the main table. The last people with canned air should bring the cans back to you.

14. When everyone is back at the main table you'll demonstrate oiling the machine's joints with the sewing machine oil. Explain that just a dot is needed since the joints are small, and they don't want oil from their machines to leak onto their fabric and stain it. Show how to turn the wheel manually while oiling to get the oil to disperse evenly over the joints.

15. Have campers head back to their tables and start oiling their machines. Let them watch other machines being oiled as a way to see how other machines operate differently than their own.

16. When they're done oiling, it's time for a little fun. Have them come up to your main table to choose a small piece of fabric and to see what your machine's setting for a straight stitch looks like.

17. Demonstrate positioning your needle to start and how to pull the threads toward the back of the machine to ensure that they aren't tangled before starting a seam.

18. Explain how to lift the foot of the machine, place the fabric in position to be sewn, and lower the foot.

19. Demonstrate smoothing the fabric and guiding it through the machine with your left hand while steering the fabric with your right hand.

20. Finally, demonstrate sewing a straight stitch. When you've completed your stitch, manually turn the wheel to position your needle to release the thread, lift your foot, and cut your threads. Show campers your even stitches on the front and back sides of your fabric.

If your stitches aren't even this is a fantastic learning opportunity! Show how you can tell they are uneven and have campers guess what to do to your tension to fix it. It's good for campers to see that even you have to keep tweaking things!

21. Have them return to their machine and set it to a straight stitch. Using the piece of fabric they should sew a straight stitch. You may want to repeat the instructions of what you just demonstrated step by step for campers to follow along. There's a good chance that with all the fun of oiling and playing with canned air their machines may have come unthreaded. Simply have them rethread the machine. Don't worry if they have to thread their machines multiple times; they'll need to know how to do it over and over again to become good sewers!

22. If time permits, have campers choose another piece of fabric and teach them how to sew the two together. They can continue sewing pieces together until it's time to clean up.

23. When 10 minutes are left in class have campers clean up their areas. Any garbage should be thrown away. Tools can be brought to your main table, and machines, manuals, and bobbins can be packed up.

24. Encourage campers to practice their straight stitch while at home this week, hand out the *Threads* magazine article on tension to everyone (for review and/or troubleshooting while practicing) and set them free!

Resources

Pre-Camp e-mail:

Hello, Camper!

I'm getting super excited for our first day of Sewing Machine Camp and wanted to touch base with you to let you know what you should bring on your first day.

- Your sewing machine!
- Your sewing machine's manual (Hopefully you still have this, but if not, check online to see if you can find a version to print out and bring with you. All machines are different, and these manuals help us understand each machine's needs and quirks.)
- Two bobbins from your machine (Bobbins are the tiny spools that hold the thread inside your machine. Sometimes they're made of metal; sometimes they're made of plastic. They don't have to have any thread on them, but if they do, that's okay too!)

I want you to know that during our first day of camp we'll be learning a lot about how your sewing machine works and getting you familiar with the basics of how it operates.

See you soon!

(Your signature)

"Understanding Thread Tension" by Claire Shaeffer from *Threads* magazine: http://www.threadsmagazine.com/item/4302/understanding -thread-tension/page/all

Stitches, Speeds, AND Troubleshooting

This lesson will teach the different stitch types available on their machines and help create a troubleshooting guide they can use when they start sewing. During the speeds lesson they'll start to become comfortable with just how fast their machines can sew and what speed they find comfortable when sewing.

Tab Indicators

STEAM

S: Experimenting with stitch types and machine to create a desired effect, hypothesizing solutions to sewing problems

T: Using a sewing machine
E: Using tools, adjusting equipment
A: Creating stitch drawings
M: Analyzing tension number settings

Time

2 hours

Age level

10 to 18 years

Ingredients

- Tables
- Chairs (one per person)
- Thread
- Seam rippers
- Sewing machine screwdrivers
- Canned air
- Machine sewing needles
- Scissors
- Cups (one per person to keep screws in)
- Computer with Internet access
- Fabric in pieces (about a square foot works best)

Setup

- Send out this week's pre-camp e-mail to let students know what to bring again. (An example is in the Resources section.)
- Read up in your sewing machine's manual about any tension changes you need to make for the special stitches your machine can do. Give it some practice and create your own stitch collage to show in camp this week.
- Set up your tables and chairs. Today campers will need room to actually sew and spread out. If you think about that 6' × 8' table again, you'll still want to seat just two people.
- Set up your main table again today for demonstration.
- Arrange thread, screwdrivers, canned air, fabric, and cups on your main table so campers have access to them but they aren't in the way.
- Evenly spread out scissors and seam rippers on tables.
- Welcome the panel of experts and thank them. Offer them water, coffee, stocks and bonds. (Just kidding.)

Instructions

1. Welcome campers back and have them choose sets again.
2. When everyone has arrived, ask them how practice went last week with their straight stitches. You may find that they ran into problems. If so, it's a perfect segue into this week's troubleshooting lesson. Explain that today you'll cover common sewing problems and how to fix them. Then later you will get into different types of stitches and their purposes.
3. First, cover what happens when your bottom thread is all loopy and tangled. This is caused by your machine being threaded incorrectly (Solution: Rethread it! Top AND bottom!) or by your top thread being too tight. (Solution: Adjust your tension!)
4. Second, go over what may cause your thread to keep breaking. This happens when you're using a needle that is the incorrect size or you put it in a little cattywhompus or crooked. (Solution: Take it out and put it back in carefully and so it is aligned properly!) It can also happen if you're trying to sew through too much fabric. (Be realistic! Try manually sewing using your wheel. If you feel resistance you may want to hand sew or slowly manually sew this area using your wheel!) Finally, you may be using the wrong foot for the stitch you chose. (Remove your fabric and watch your needle as you manually sew using the wheel. Is the needle hitting the foot? If so, replace it with the correct foot! Your manual should tell you which foot goes with which stitch.)
5. The final typical problem we encounter when sewing is uneven stitches that look like they "skip." (Usually it means it's time for a new needle. Replace your needle with a nice, sharp, new one and you should see improvement!)
6. Now it's time for some fun! Give a quick demonstration of how the speed of your machine works. Be sure to explain that many people think sewing fast means sewing well, but there are fine movements you simply can't perform going at breakneck speeds!
7. Encourage campers to return to their machines and test out their machine's speeds and their own personal comfort zones.
8. After a testing period, call campers back up to the main table, it's time for stitch collages! Show your premade stitch collage and demonstrate a few of the cool stitches on your own machine. Remember to highlight stitches that you need to adjust the tension to properly use.
9. Have students choose a piece of fabric and go back to their machines. It's time for them to experiment with the stitches offered on their own machines. Expect some of those troubleshooting issues to arise and to help campers deal with them.

10. When campers have successfully completed a collage they are happy with, challenge them to write their names using the stitch pattern of their choice. This will build even more familiarity with how their machines work and what speed they are comfortable sewing with.
11. Allow campers to make as many stitch collages as they would like. Encourage their enjoyment and any crazy ideas they may have.
12. When they have two collages, have them come up to the main table so you can show them (in small groups or solo) how to sew two pieces of fabric together. You'll want to discuss:
   • Putting "right" sides together
   • Locking stitches at the beginning and end
   • "Serging" the edge of the fabric without a serger by using a zig-zag stitch
13. After you've demonstrated this, have them return to their own machines and give it a try!
14. When 10 minutes are left in class have campers clean up their areas. Any garbage should be thrown away. Tools can be brought to your main table, and their machines, manuals, and bobbins can be packed up.
15. Encourage campers to practice their various stitches at home this week and set them free!

Resources

Good books on sewing:

One-Yard Wonders: 101 Sewing Fabric Projects; Look How Much You Can Make with Just One Yard of Fabric! by Rebecca Yaker and Patricia Hoskins (ISBN 1603424490)

A Kid's Guide to Sewing: Learn to Sew with Sophie & Her Friends; 16 Fun Projects You'll Love to Make & Use by Sophie Kerr and Weeks Ringle (ISBN 1607057512)

Pre-Camp e-mail:

Hello, Camper!

This week we're going to be experimenting with stitches, with the speed of our machines, and learning how to solve common sewing problems. You'll want to bring in

• Your sewing machine!
• Your sewing machine's manual
• Two bobbins from your machine

Get ready to discover your inner fabric artist this week!

(Your signature)

Fabric Petting Zoo

Now that campers have a good feel for both their capabilities and their machine's capabilities, it's time to have some fun learning about fabric's role in sewing. The variations that need to be made between a thin silk and a corduroy can break a budding sewer's heart as well as needles if not tackled properly. Experimenting on different fabrics will prepare your campers for a multitude of projects. On top of learning the final step they'll need to venture out into the world ready to start sewing, they'll also give creating a project a try. It's a great lesson for kids to simply imagine something they'd like to create and just give it a whirl. We don't always need patterns to make things, and we don't always have to get things right on the first try. Teaching this to your sewers early on will be a great gift to them as they venture out after camp into their own unique sewing worlds!

Tab Indicators

STEAM

- S: Experimenting with equipment and tools for desired outcomes, hypothesizing solutions to sewing problems
- T: Using a sewing machine
- E: Using tools, adjusting equipment, manipulating equipment manually, learning and utilizing different strategies for sewing with varying materials
- A: Imagining a project and attempting to bring it to life
- M: Analyzing tension number settings

Time

2 hours

Age level

10 to 18 years

Ingredients

- Tables
- Chairs (one per person)

- Thread
- A wide variety of fabric (satin, silk, tulle, netting, cotton, muslin, T-shirts or jersey knits, lamé, spandex, whatever you can get your hands on!)
- Seam rippers
- Scrap paper
- Pencils or pens
- Sewing machine screwdrivers
- Canned air
- Scissors
- Cups (one per person to keep screws in)
- Fabric markers (one for two campers should be enough)
- Measuring tapes (one for every two campers should be enough)
- Pins

Setup

- If there's something in particular that you can make that doesn't require a pattern—do it! Your campers will love seeing real-life examples of things you were able to imagine and then bring to life. Some wow factor items that always seem to please are tutus, monster dolls, and jewelry.
- Prepare slips of paper with numbers 1 through however many campers you have. Fold them up and put them in something that you can use later for a random drawing.
- Set up your tables and chairs. Today, campers will need room to actually sew and spread out. If you think about that six × eight foot table again, you'll still want to seat just two people.
- Set up your main table again today for demonstration.
- Arrange the scrap paper, writing utensils, fabric, thread, screwdrivers, canned air, fabric, and cups on your main table so campers have access to them but they aren't in the way.
- Evenly spread out scissors and seam rippers, pins, batting, measuring tapes and fabric markers on tables.
- Welcome the panel of experts and thank them. Offer them water and/or coffee.

Instructions

1. Welcome campers and invite them to get their machines set up.
2. When they're all set up they can join you at the main table so you can show your examples of fun projects you've made without patterns. Explain that today they'll each be getting a piece of fabric they can do whatever they want with.

3. Have campers draw a number at random and hold on to it.

4. Showing off the fabric you'll explain today's challenge: first, they will choose their unique piece of fabric; second, they will test some stitches and techniques out on a sample piece of the fabric; and third, they will make something that can fit in a shoebox out of their fabric.

5. Have the camper with the number 1 come up and choose his or her piece of fabric first, then number 2, and so on.

6. Invite campers to grab some scrap paper and writing utensils and start drawing out their own creations.

7. After they have a design they're happy with, have them use their manuals to see if they can find instructions on the proper setting to sew with using the fabric they chose. If they don't have such a section it's not a big deal. Share the following info with them on what thread to choose. Encourage them to start with their standard settings and troubleshoot their way to their machine's personal sweet spot for the fabric they chose. Here are some tips about picking the right thread for their fabrics:

   • Lightweight fabrics (thin cotton, voile, tulle, silk, muslin, jerseys, knits, crepes) should use a light-duty cotton, polyester, or nylon thread.

   • Medium-weight fabrics (heavier knit, thicker cottons, spandex, satin, lightweight wool, sail cloth) can use most threads and should use the same thread on both the top and bottom.

   • Heavy-weight fabrics (canvas, wool, quilted fabrics, tent material, denim, upholstery material) should use the same thread on top and bottom and can use a wide variety of threads.

   • Very heavy fabrics (leather, wool, vinyl) should use a heavy thread or carpet thread and will require increased tension on the top thread.

8. Now it's time to cut a test piece out of their fabric that's large enough to sew on.

9. Using this scrap piece they should adjust their tension settings and then sew a sample stitch. If their tension looks good and there aren't any problems to troubleshoot they can go forth and start creating their masterpiece! As always, you'll remain available to help troubleshoot, offer advice, and cheerlead. As you're wandering around helping, don't forget to keep them up to date on the amount of time they have remaining for creation. Their creation doesn't have to be finished during today's class, but they will need to show off their progress and share their findings.

10. When there are 30 minutes left in your session, have the campers show off their designs and share their tips (regarding tension, settings, and speed) about working with the fabric they chose.

11. With 10 minutes remaining, they should start cleaning up to go home.
12. Hand out printed copies of the resources so they can continue their explorations at home.
13. When there are 5 minutes left in class, have them give you feedback! They can either write it down on the scrap paper lying around if they want to be anonymous or they can simply tell you what they liked and didn't like. You may need to lead the conversation, but take what they say to heart. A good question to end with is whether or not they'd like to do this again.

Resources

Some great info on choosing the right needle by Sarah: http://www.sewingpartsonline.com/blog/which-sewing-machine-needle-to-use/

Good advice on choosing fabric for your clothes projects: http://www.craftsy.com/blog/2013/10/choosing-fabric-for-clothes/

Cool Infographic on choosing the right needle for your project by sewingpartsonline.com

http://www.sewingpartsonline.com/blog/finding-perfect-sewing-machine-needle-infographic/

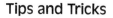

Tips and Tricks

- This camp may seem intimidating to new sewers or folks who haven't sewn in a long time. It shouldn't be! With some practice and giving the lessons a whirl ahead of time, anyone can teach these lessons. If you're still feeling unsure you could always look to hire someone to teach the lessons you're uncomfortable with. Some grants even have room for hiring others. Places like local sewing centers and shops are a great place to start looking.
- When starting this camp you may want to have a small class size. Without the certainty of obtaining a panel of experts, you could wind up doing a lot of the helping yourself, and while you're off helping one camper things could go wrong with the others, creating a bottleneck. If it's just you teaching consider starting with four or five campers in a smaller age range. If that goes well you can always add more ages or campers next time, but it's better to start small and build off your success and good reputation than to aim high and fail, tarnishing your program's reputation.

- You may encounter parents who want their children younger than 10 to be able to attend camp. I would advise against this. At its very easiest and best there is a lot of rethreading that goes on with sewing. Without the dexterity to rethread easily, the activities you're participating in will be frustrating to young children. If a parent is willing to be the child's personal helper, you may consider it, but beware of parents who are looking to participate and learn sewing for themselves. If you find there's a great call for this kind of program for adults, feel free to adapt it for that age group. The framework provided should work just the same.

These high-level learning experiences have been a big hit here in Chattanooga. I'm planning a whole series of them for my summer programming this year in lieu of the traditional summer reading game. While they can be a lot of work, they also produce some of the best feedback from teens I've ever received. Recently, at my Etsy camp one teen told me that she realized the other day that camp was almost as long as school, but she previously had no idea because she loves camp so much and waits for it all week.

As I've mentioned over and over again, you should get feedback from your patrons and plan your future programming based on that, not what's hot in the library world. Our communities are all different and deserve the very best that we can give them. Luckily, our programming will continue to be different, we'll continue to share with one another, and we'll continue to pass that on to our lucky patrons. You're going to rock this!

INDEX

After Party (volunteers), 118–120
Alternative Looms (recipe),
    19–21
antiprogramming, 1–14, 18–19, 54,
    56
Art Station (recipe), 11–13

bubonic plague, 31–32
Buddha Board (recipe), 7–9
Button Maker (recipe), 5–7

Chattanooga Public Library, 3, 5,
    62, 116, 127, 175, 179
community
    partnerships, 99, 124, 125, 126,
        137, 143–157, 160–164, 168,
        172
    service. *See* volunteers
cooking club, 83–98
The Corpse Bride, 127

crime scene investigation (CSI),
    99–112
    fingerprint station, 104–106
    pH station, 103
    shoe print station, 103
Cyborg Pinup Flowers and Cyborg
    Feltie Pins (recipe), 48–52

Darth Double Dogs, 93–97
decorating, 124, 126–127, 129, 130,
    132–133, 140
Design (recipe), 65–67
Design Your Own Rainbow Loom
    Video (recipe), 23–26
digital
    creation, 3, 23
    consumption, 3, 23
    divide, 3
Divergent, 128, 130–131, 133,
    136–137, 139–140

Disgusting Human Body (recipe),
    30–33
Disgusting Science, 29–45
donations, 13
Dream Big (recipe), 67–69
Duplicate (recipe), 60–65

electronics
    currents, 50
    wearable, 47, 48–53

Fabric Petting Zoo (recipe), 171–174
farts, 32, 34, 44, 45, 73, 76
Fingerprint Analysis, 101, 102,
    104–105, 107, 111
    worksheet, 108
focus groups, 14, 113–122
Footprint Analysis, 101, 102, 106,
    111
    worksheet, 110

glass etching. See Minecraft Glass
    Etching

Harry Potter, 124, 128, 130
Hunger Games, 125, 127, 130

Instagram Photo Booth (recipe),
    3–5
internships, 143–157

Java Jive Milk Shakes, 88–92

LEDs, 47, 48 (photo), 50–52
    (photo), 57
Legos, 62, 70, 71–81
The Lord of the Rings, 128

Makerspaces, 1, 3, 18, 23, 128
Marvel, 123, 124, 128, 130

Minecraft, 17, 47, 48, 62
Minecraft Glass Etching (recipe),
    53–56
    worksheet, 58
movie events, 122, 123–141
    worksheets, 132, 134–135, 138

One-Hour Build-Off (recipe),
    77–79

passive programming. See
    Antiprogramming
pH, 100, 102, 104, 105–106, 111
    worksheet, 108
photo booth, 2, 3–5
Pinterest, 2, 3, 128, 131
programming statistics, 1, 19

rainbow looms, 14, 15–27, 55, 119
Rainbow Loom Antiprogram
    (recipe), 18–19
Recreate a Human Stomach
    (recipe), 33–37
    worksheet, 38

Science behind Vampires (recipe),
    39–42
    worksheet, 43–44
Sewing
    electronics, wearable, 157
    machine camp, 159–175
60-Second Lego Challenge (recipe),
    72–75
Spangler, Steve, 32, 33
Star Wars, 81, 83–98, 115
STEAM, 3–4, 5, 8–10, 12, 18, 21, 24,
    30, 33–34, 39, 49, 53–54, 61, 66,
    68, 73, 77, 85, 89, 93–94, 102,
    114–115, 118, 130, 147–148, 162,
    167–168, 171

Stitches, Speeds, AND Trouble-
    shooting (recipe), 167–171
stomach, 33–37

teen advisory boards, 113. *See also*
    focus groups
teen advisory groups. *See* focus
    groups
teen employment, 143–157
Teenage Mutant Ninja Turtles, 128,
    130
Teen Opportunities Fair,
    147–154
Threading, Tension, and Anatomy
    and Care of a Sewing Machine
    (recipe), 162–167
3D Printer, 16, 57, 59–70, 119

unprogramming. *See*
    antiprogramming

volunteers
    management, 126, 129–130,
        138–140, 141, 150–151, 163,
        168, 172
    opportunities, 2, 15, 72, 86,
        143–157
    programs, 21–23
    recognition, 118–120, 151
    recruitment, 150
Volunteer-Led Rainbow Loom
    Class (recipe), 21–23

Yarn Bombing (recipe), 2, 9–11
Yoda Soda (recipe), 84–88

About the Author

MEGAN EMERY SCHADLICH works at the Chattanooga Public Library in Chattanooga, Tennessee. She holds a degree in adventure recreation from Green Mountain College, Poultney, Vermont. Her blog is at www. meganfemery.com.